BEYOND WINGS & FEATHERS

DEDICATIONS

To my beloved mother, Parin Lakhani for sparking my passion for mysticism, spiritual enlightenment, and knowledge.

To my beloved Wife, Riya, whose unwavering support is my anchor, and to our cherished Daughter, Aylin, whose innocence and joy inspire me every day.

To my dear Sisters, Shamim, Pinki, and Minaz, your support and guidance have been a steady presence in my life's journey, shaping me into who I am today.

Lastly, to the invaluable teachers, mentors and colleagues who have illuminated my path, coaching me and nurturing the flame of my potential, your unwavering encouragement has been the wind beneath my wings.

IN LOVING MEMORY OF

MUSTAKALI LAKHANI
(D. JUNE, 2010)

My Beloved Dad,

Across the passage of time, your influence remains a constant presence in our journeys. As I navigate the complexities of life, your guidance brings me comfort. Your wisdom serves as a guiding light, illuminating the path ahead. With every page I turn, your legacy unfolds, revealing the valuable insights you've shared. Your values have firmly taken root in my heart, blossoming into virtues that I carry with me. Your love shines through these words, demonstrating how one person's soul can deeply impact another's life. In my intellectual explorations, your torch of knowledge continues to burn brightly, guiding me as I search for meaning beyond the everyday. Despite your physical absence, our ethereal connection transcends this world. I feel your essence in every sentence and every thought within the pages of this book.

In the celestial realms, may your soul find tranquility. Your memory lingers as a benevolent force, propelling me to seek a deeper understanding. Your lessons persist: valuing wisdom over mere facts and nurturing curiosity over stagnant knowledge. With profound gratitude, I bid you farewell. Your legacy lives on through my pursuit of knowledge and understanding. You remain an integral part of my story, guiding me through the vast realm of human thought.

With love and reverence,
Your loving son

BEYOND WINGS & FEATHERS

Exploring Spiritual Allegory and Quest for Truth from Attar's Conference of the Birds

AMIN LAKHANI

PARIAY PUBLISHERS

Paperback & electronic editions published in 2023 by

PARIAY PUBLISHERS
St. Thomas, ON Canada

ISBN (paperback) 978-1-7380159-0-0
ISBN (electronic) 978-1-7380159-1-7

Copyright © 2023 by PARIAY PUBLISHERS

First published in 2023 by PARIAY PUBLISHERS

All rights reserved. Except for brief quotations in a review, this book or any part thereof, may not be reproduced in any form without permission in writing from the publisher.

PREFACE

In the intricate weave of human existence, where threads of both the tangible and intangible interlace to form intricate patterns, a dimension beyond our immediate perceptions comes to light. This dimension is a realm where allegory intertwines with truth, where the relentless pursuit of comprehension takes flight on the wings of spirituality. "Beyond Wings and Feathers" embodies the culmination of my lifelong exploration through these dimensions—a journey that was initiated as a gift from my beloved mother and evolved into a quest of profound spiritual discovery, scholarly inquiry, and an unbreakable bond with the age-old poem known as Fariduddin Attar's "Conference of the Birds."

My voyage into the enigmatic passages of Attar's masterpiece began long before I set ink to paper for this book. In 1998, when I was a student educator, I embarked upon a path dedicated to imparting spiritual wisdom within my community, sparking the flames of introspection and sagacity in the hearts of those I served. During those formative days, my mother, who possessed wisdom beyond measure, introduced me to the captivating realm of the "Conference of the Birds." Her guidance turned the allegorical tales and spiritual lessons within the poem from mere textual arrangements into a living panorama of insight and motivation.

From those nascent moments, a seed was planted deep within me—a seed that sprouted into an insatiable curiosity for the mystical, a yearning to unveil the intricate layers of meaning intricately entwined within every verse of Attar's creation. As time progressed, this fascination evolved into an unwavering commitment. In 2007, I took a definitive stance: I was embarking on a literary expedition to distill the essence of Attar's "Conference of the Birds" and to disseminate its profound teachings across the globe.

The subsequent years were marked by unyielding devotion to the pursuit of wisdom, an unflagging determination to comprehend the depths of mysticism, and an insatiable thirst for enlightenment. This book, the outcome of that expedition, aspires to convey not only my personal interpretations of the epic poem but also to delve into the diverse viewpoints that have flourished in academic circles. It stands as a testament to the richness of Attar's creation, which has fostered a plethora of perspectives, each offering a distinct glimpse into the realms of spirituality and veracity.

Although this book undoubtedly provides my insights and analyses, it extends beyond mere academia. It acts as a bridge between the arcane and the comprehensible, a sincere endeavor to render the intricate wisdom of Attar into language that resonates with both scholars and seekers. Attar's work, often veiled in non-English languages, academic discourses, or concealed within poetic metaphors, has remained elusive to the general populace. Through this undertaking, my intention is to breathe vitality into these timeless teachings, rendering them approachable and impactful for all those who are inclined to embark on this expedition of revelation.

In "Beyond Wings and Feathers," I cordially invite you to join me on a transformative quest—a spiritual pilgrimage guided by allegorical avian beings, a pursuit of truth that surpasses the confines of time and cultural borders. It is my fervent wish that this book may serve as a lantern, illuminating the path for those who seek, a wellspring of sagacity for those who contemplate, and a celebration of the immeasurable wisdom enshrined within Attar's ageless creation.

May the winds of curiosity carry you forward, and may the ensuing pages become a vessel for your own expedition into the heart of mysticism, truth, and self-discovery.

With genuine anticipation,
Amin Lakhani

INTRODUCTION

Fariduddin Attar, one of the most celebrated Persian poets, was born in Nishapur in the 12th century. Known for his profound mystical and philosophical insights, Attar's works have left an indelible mark on Islamic literature, particularly within the Sufi tradition. Among his many contributions, "Conference of the Birds" ("Mantiq al-Tayr") stands as a timeless masterpiece, weaving allegory, poetry, and spiritual wisdom into an epic tale that resonates across cultures and epochs.

"Conference of the Birds" is an allegorical poem that encapsulates a spiritual journey towards enlightenment and self-realization. It narrates the tale of birds, each symbolizing different human characteristics and moral attributes, embarking on a quest to find the Simorgh, their mythical king. Guided by the hoopoe, a symbol of wisdom and spiritual guidance, the birds traverse through seven treacherous valleys, each representing a stage in the spiritual path.

The poem begins with the birds of the world recognizing their need for a king and seeking the guidance of the hoopoe to lead them to the Simorgh. Their journey, however, is fraught with hesitations, excuses, and fears, reflecting the internal battles that humans face on their spiritual paths. Through their dialogues, Attar explores themes of love, intellectual inquiry, detachment, unity, humility, and self-annihilation, painting a vivid picture of the human soul's quest for the divine.

One of the most remarkable aspects of "Conference of the Birds" is Attar's use of symbolism. The birds, valleys, and even the name "Simorgh" are laden with metaphorical meanings, providing layers of interpretation. The birds' excuses to avoid the journey mirror common human faults, such as vanity, greed, fear, and attachment to worldly pleasures. The hoopoe's rebuttals, filled with wisdom and insights, serve as spiritual teachings that guide not only the birds but also the readers through their personal journeys towards self-awareness and spiritual enlightenment.

The seven valleys that the birds must traverse are allegorical representations of the stages of spiritual growth. From the initial quest to the final realization of unity and annihilation of the self, the valleys are a roadmap for spiritual seekers. They challenge, enlighten, and transform the birds, reflecting the transformative power of the spiritual path.

Far from being merely a tale for the spiritually inclined, "Conference of the Birds" is also a rich literary work filled with poetic beauty, wit, and psychological insight. It speaks to the human condition, offering timeless wisdom on love, loss, ambition, fear, and the endless pursuit of meaning. Attar's poetry transcends cultural and religious boundaries, speaking to the universal human experience.

Despite its ancient origins, "Conference of the Birds" continues to be a relevant and inspiring work in contemporary times. It has been translated into numerous languages, adapted into plays, and inspired artwork and music. Its universal themes and profound wisdom resonate with readers from various backgrounds, making it a valuable resource for scholars, spiritual seekers, and literary enthusiasts alike.

Fariduddin Attar's "Conference of the Birds" is a monumental work that skillfully intertwines allegory, poetry, and spiritual philosophy. Its exploration of the human soul's journey towards the divine, encapsulated in the symbolic narrative of birds seeking their king, makes it a timeless masterpiece that continues to inspire and enlighten. Whether approached as a spiritual guide, a literary treasure, or a reflection on human nature, "Conference of the Birds" offers a rich and multifaceted reading experience, affirming Attar's place as one of the great literary and spiritual masters of all time.

CONTENTS

Preface vii
Introduction ix

1. Seeking the Simorgh: An Ethereal Journey of Oneness, Self-Exploration, and Moral Aspiration   1

OBSTACLES AND EXCUSES: REFLECTING THE HUMAN CONDITION   7

2. The Nightingale's Dilemma: Love, Attachment, and Spiritual Quest   10

3. Reflections of Desire: Unveiling Spiritual Truths in the Dialogue between the Parrot and the Hoopoe   13

4. Unmasking Pride and Embracing Humility: The Dialogue Between the Peacock and the Hoopoe   18

5. Beyond Attachment: The Dialogue Between the Duck and the Hoopoe   23

6. Unveiling the Illusion: The Owl's Treasure and the Path to Spiritual Awakening   27

7. Transcending Earthly Bonds: The Dialogue Between the Falcon and the Hoopoe   30

8. Embracing the Abyss: The Dialogue Between the Heron and the Hoopoe   35

| 9 | Guiding Light: Role of the Hoopoe as a Spiritual Guide | 39 |

THE SEVEN VALLEYS ... **43**

10	Embarking on the Spiritual Odyssey: Unveiling Wisdom of the Valley of Quest	44
11	Transcending Boundaries: An In-Depth Exploration of the Valley of Love	66
12	Transcending the Superficial: A Comprehensive Exploration of the Valley of Knowledge	79
13	Valley of Detachment: A Symbol of Cultivating the Inner Richness	95
14	Valley of Unity: A symbol of Spiritual Realization	101
15	Valley of Bewilderment: Transition from the comfort of the known to the excitement of discovery	110
16	Valley of Annihilation and Nothingness: Embracing Divine Unity and Practical Wisdom	129

MEETING THE SIMORGH ... **161**

| 17 | Celestial Encounter: The Birds' Meeting with the Simorgh | 162 |

Bibiliography ... 165

CHAPTER 1

Seeking the Simorgh: An Ethereal Journey of Oneness, Self-Exploration, and Moral Aspiration

The poem opens with a gathering of birds from diverse backgrounds and lands, symbolizing the diversity of human experiences and perspectives. They convene in a valley, facing the guidance of the hoopoe, a bird of wisdom and experience. The hoopoe introduces the central quest: to find their true sovereign, the Simorgh. This figure represents the divine reality, the ultimate truth to which the birds are drawn.

Initially, the birds respond with skepticism and uncertainty, mirroring the human condition of doubt and confusion in matters of spirituality. They voice concerns and hesitations about embarking on this journey. The hoopoe, assuming the role of a spiritual guide, addresses their doubts with sagacious advice and motivational encouragement. The birds are implored to transcend their apprehensions and initiate a transformative spiritual expedition to discover the Simorgh.

The hoopoe further narrates the tale of undertaking a mission as King Solomon's emissary. Hoopoe's task is to convey a letter to the Queen of Sheba. Throughout this journey, Hoopoe is exposed to the wonders and marvels of the world, symbolizing the allure of worldly distractions and experiences.

Upon arriving in the land of Sheba and meeting the Queen, Hoopoe realizes that despite her opulent worldly existence, she remains ignorant of the deeper spiritual truths. The Queen and her subjects worship the sun, signifying their attachment to material symbols rather than recognizing the ultimate source of existence. Hoopoe's story functions as an allegory to emphasize the futility of pursuing materialistic desires and highlights the need to seek a profound, spiritual understanding. This lays the groundwork for the overarching narrative of the birds' journey towards enlightenment. The wise hoopoe's role as a spiritual guide becomes evident as he shares insightful stories that aim to inspire the birds to overcome their uncertainties. Their quest for self-discovery and connection with the divine is at the core of the poem's philosophy.

As the story unfolds, the characters and themes introduced in these initial chapters will evolve, offering deeper insights into Sufi thought, the nature of spirituality, and the intricacies of the human soul. "The Conference of the Birds" invites readers to explore profound philosophical concepts through its rich allegorical storytelling.

Hoopoe's guidance establishes the essential framework for the allegorical expedition of the birds. This voyage serves as a symbolic representation of an intense spiritual longing and the pursuit of a profound link with the divine. The allegory draws striking comparisons between the birds' odyssey and humanity's pursuit of self-exploration, enlightenment, and the ultimate unity with the divine.

The gathering of birds mirrors the diversity of human experiences, desires, and longings. Just as the birds assemble with different appearances and voices, humanity too is composed of diverse individuals seeking meaning and purpose. The Hoopoe, representing spiritual wisdom and guidance, addresses the birds' longing for a king, a metaphor for the human yearning for spiritual guidance and a higher purpose. This initial longing reflects the innate human desire to connect with something greater than oneself, to seek answers to life's existential questions, and to find a source of meaning and unity. The birds' collective aspiration for a king mirrors humanity's universal search for a transcendent truth that can provide guidance and direction in a complex world.

The birds' responses to the Hoopoe's call illustrate the various ways individuals respond to their spiritual yearning. Just as the birds come forward with different emotions and motivations, humans too possess a range of attitudes when it comes to their pursuit of the divine. Some birds, exemplify passion and courage, symbolizing those who are willing to passionately seek the truth despite challenges. The Hoopoe's guidance, cautioning about the difficulties of the journey, mirrors the guidance provided by spiritual mentors or teachings in real life. This guidance acknowledges the trials that individuals encounter on the path to self-discovery and enlightenment, emphasizing that the spiritual journey is not without its challenges. Ultimately, the quest for the Simorgh represents the profound spiritual yearning inherent in human beings. Just as the birds are driven by an irresistible longing to find their king, humans possess an innate urge to seek a deeper understanding of themselves and their place in the universe. The Simorgh's symbolism as a divine and mysterious being resonates with the idea of the ultimate truth or God that individuals yearn to unite with. The birds' willingness to embark on a transformative journey, despite the challenges and uncertainties, mirrors the courage and determination required of individuals who pursue spiritual growth. As the birds set out on their path, they signify the human resolve to confront their limitations, detach from worldly attachments, and overcome obstacles in order to attain a higher state of consciousness and connect with the divine.

The willingness to embark on the journey symbolizes the profound spiritual yearning and quest for connection with the divine that is inherent in human nature. The allegory captures the diversity of human responses, the need for spiritual guidance, and the challenges individuals encounter on their journey towards self-discovery, enlightenment, and union with the ultimate truth. The search for the Simorgh symbolizes a profound spiritual yearning. It represents the universal human desire to connect with a higher power or divine source. The birds, each embodying different aspects of human nature, feel a void in their existence. They seek to fill this void by embarking on a journey to find the Simorgh, which embodies the Divine in Sufi tradition.

In the realm of Sufism, the pursuit of the Divine takes on the profound analogy of a voyage towards ultimate truth. The birds' relentless search for the enigmatic Simorgh is not a mere expedition to locate a monarch; instead, it embodies a profound revelation of their authentic essence, forging a connection with the Divine that soars above terrestrial confines. This expedition necessitates the birds to transcend their personal egos and individual aspirations, urging them onto a path of spiritual metamorphosis. This path, laden with the essence of self-surrender, beckons them to embrace a more expansive and enlightened outlook.

The birds' relentless journey toward a sovereign figure is fueled by an innate yearning for unity and coherence. Within each avian entity resides a representation of distinct human qualities and shortcomings. Their collective aspiration for a sovereign being mirrors a quest to converge and infuse their existence with purpose and direction. The Simorgh's pursuit stands as a profound allegory for the quest for shared identity and a communal sense of significance. This yearning for a cohesive entity or principle is a universally shared human experience, particularly in a world brimming with diversity. Beneath the wings of the quest for the Simorgh lies a communal aspiration for advancement and evolution. This pursuit epitomizes the shared journey toward heightened comprehension, sagacity, and enlightenment, a path frequented by humanity.

Acknowledgment of their requisite for a sovereign figure symbolizes the birds' acute awareness of their own limitations. They confront their vulnerabilities head-on, seeking sagacity to transcend these very limitations. Each bird personifies an array of human frailties like greed, pride, vanity, and fear. Their eagerness to embark on this expedition conveys an acceptance of these imperfections and an earnest yearning to surmount them. In the guise of the Hoopoe, their sagacious guide, the emblem of wisdom and spiritual insight is portrayed. The pursuit of the Simorgh comes to exemplify the transformative potency of guidance, an expedition that meanders from ignorance toward enlightenment, from division to unity.

Beyond its surface narrative, the pursuit of the Simorgh unveils a metaphorical odyssey toward self-discovery. It unearths a profound quest to unearth one's genuine self, liberated from superficial identities and attachments. This journey, inherently intrinsic, urges readers to undertake their personal expeditions of self-exploration, to delve within, and recognize the divine essence residing therein.

Embedded in the Sufi tradition is the expedition towards self-realization, a journey often necessitating the dissolution of the self, a relinquishment of ego and individuality to meld with the Divine. The birds' relentless search mirrors this profound spiritual evolution. Their quest for the Simorgh can also be interpreted as a response to an existential quandary. A sense of emptiness, void, and a lack of purpose instigate their quest for a sovereign figure, to fill this void with meaning. This pursuit reverberates as a universal human ache for answers to existential quandaries concerning existence, identity, and reality. It taps into the profound existential quandaries that have beguiled humanity across epochs. Attar, through the birds' voyage, delves into philosophical musings about free will, destiny, and the fundamental nature of reality. Their pursuit transmutes into a profound philosophical exploration, rendering the poem an ageless meditation on human existence.

On a societal echelon, the quest for a sovereign figure unfurls as a call for moral and ethical unity. The Simorgh embodies an archetype, a pinnacle of virtue and sagacity, toward which the community endeavors. The search for the Simorgh mirrors a collective aspiration for elevated ethical precepts, a shared moral compass steering individual and communal conduct. The pursuit of a sovereign figure equally embodies a yearning for ethical leadership, a leadership that embodies sagacity, compassion, and integrity, steering society toward justice and harmony.

The poem, hence, is a rich and complex allegory that delves into the human psyche, spirituality, ethics, and philosophy. The birds' quest for their king, the Simorgh, is a multifaceted symbol that captures the complexities and aspirations of the human soul. It is a universal narrative that transcends cultural and temporal boundaries, reflecting a timeless exploration of human nature and existence. Whether it's the spiritual quest for connection, the desire for unity and purpose, the recognition of imperfection, the metaphor for self-realization, the response to existential crises, or the longing for social and ethical cohesion, the search for the king embodies the multifarious dimensions of human life, making "The Conference of the Birds" a profound and enduring masterpiece.

Obstacles and Excuses: Reflecting the Human Condition

In "The Conference of the Birds," Attar masterfully weaves a tapestry of excuses presented by the birds when confronted with the notion of embarking on a journey to find the Simorgh, their true king. Each excuse resonates deeply with the human experience, shedding light on the myriad doubts and obstacles individuals encounter when faced with the prospect of spiritual seeking and personal transformation.

One prominent theme that emerges from the birds' excuses is the reluctance to leave their familiar nests and habitats. This reluctance mirrors the human tendency to cling to comfort zones and resist change. Just as some birds feared abandoning their accustomed environments, many individuals find themselves trapped in routines and comfort zones, even when those circumstances hinder their personal growth.

The unknown challenges of the journey struck fear and hesitation into the hearts of certain birds. This apprehension mirrors the common human fear of stepping into uncharted territories, both in the external world and within oneself. The fear of the unknown can paralyze individuals, preventing them from embracing new experiences and opportunities for transformation.

Some birds, engrossed in their immediate desires for sustenance or sensory pleasures, serve as a reflection of how attachments to worldly desires can divert attention from spiritual pursuits This attachment to material and sensory gratification is a common obstacle on the path of self-discovery, often leading individuals away from the pursuit of higher truths and inner growth.

The concerns about survival expressed by certain birds, including worries about predators and harsh conditions during the journey, resonate with human anxieties about security in times of personal or spiritual change. These concerns highlight the innate human desire for safety and stability, which can deter individuals from taking risks and embracing transformative journeys.

In addition to these concerns, a few birds expressed doubts about the very existence of the Simorgh or the feasibility of the journey itself. This skepticism mirrors the internal struggles people often face regarding the existence of higher truths or the effectiveness of spiritual practices. Such doubts can create intellectual barriers that obstruct the path to enlightenment.

Meanwhile, some birds seemed oblivious to the significance of the Simorgh and the potential rewards of the journey due to a lack of awareness or understanding. This serves as a reminder that spiritual seeking often requires a deep understanding of one's purpose and a recognition of the profound benefits that can be gained through inner transformation.

Certain birds cited responsibilities and obligations that prevented them from embarking on the journey, echoing how people often prioritize daily duties and worldly obligations over spiritual quests. This reflects the challenges individuals face in balancing their worldly responsibilities with their inner yearnings for spiritual growth.

Collectively, these excuses painted by Attar offer profound insights into the human condition when confronted with the call for self-discovery and spiritual growth. They mirror the doubts, attachments, and challenges that can hinder individuals from embarking on a profound journey of inner transformation. The Hoopoe, in responding to these excuses, serves as a guiding light, inspiring both the birds within the story and readers outside it to rise above these barriers and undertake the transformative journey toward enlightenment and unity with the divine. "The Conference of the Birds" thus stands as a timeless allegory, inviting us all to contemplate and overcome the obstacles that lie in our own paths to self-discovery and spiritual awakening.

In the upcoming chapters, we will delve into the various excuses presented by the bird pilgrims, examining their relevance to modern seekers. Additionally, we will closely examine how the Hoopoe skillfully counters these excuses, motivating and persuading the birds to participate in the quest for the ultimate goal, the Simorgh.

CHAPTER 2

The Nightingale's Dilemma: Love, Attachment, and Spiritual Quest

Upon learning about the upcoming challenges they would face on their impending journey, a deep conversation unfolds between the Nightingale and the Hoopoe. This dialogue dives into the intricacies of human emotions, the desire for spiritual growth, and the search for profound divine understanding. The Nightingale's explanation revolves around his intense love for the Rose and serves as a captivating exploration of the human journey, touching on themes of attachment, love, and the pursuit of a higher spiritual calling. He justifies his reluctance by declaring that his connection with the Rose consumes him entirely, providing his life with meaning and beauty. According to him, this love is his path to the divine, a spiritual connection that binds him to the material world while also transcending it.

The decision to forego the journey to find the Simorgh, a symbol of divine truth, symbolizes the powerful attachment humans have to the material world. The Nightingale's passionate love for the Rose is depicted as an all-encompassing force that fills his existence with meaning and beauty. He argues that this love is his spiritual connection, blurring the line between the worldly and the divine. This portrayal of the Nightingale's love for the Rose illustrates the human tendency to perceive the divine in the physical realm and to find spiritual significance in earthly relationships. The Nightingale's perspective reflects how individuals often become absorbed in worldly beauty and pleasure, mistaking them for the ultimate truth.

The Hoopoe, symbolizing wisdom and spiritual guidance, acknowledges the sincerity of the Nightingale's love but challenges its limitations. He argues that the Nightingale's love for the Rose is fleeting, tied to physical beauty and worldly pleasure. It's a love that restricts and binds rather than liberates and enlightens. The Hoopoe counters the Nightingale's justification by pointing out that true love is not confined to a specific object or form; it seeks the eternal and the absolute. True love, he teaches, transcends physical appearance and seeks the essence. It's a love that dissolves attachments and leads to the realization of the One, the ultimate truth. He urges the Nightingale to recognize the impermanent nature of his love for the Rose, to look beyond physical beauty, and to embark on the journey toward an eternal love that transcends form and impermanence.

This dialogue between the Nightingale and the Hoopoe offers profound lessons for readers. The Nightingale's love for the Rose symbolizes humanity's inclination to cling to earthly beauty and pleasures. It serves as a reminder of how easy it is to become entangled in the allure of the physical world and mistake it for true spiritual connection. The Hoopoe's rebuttal teaches the importance of transcending earthly attachments and seeking a higher, more eternal form of love. It challenges readers to question their attachments and encourages them to seek a love that goes beyond the confines of form and impermanence. The dialogue underscores the essence of spiritual pursuit, emphasizing the search for the Divine rather than attachment to specific manifestations of the divine. It illustrates the journey from love of the particular to love of the universal, from attachment to liberation.

The wisdom of the Hoopoe and his guidance provide insights into the nature of spiritual mentorship. They demonstrate how wise counsel can illuminate the path, challenge limitations, and guide seekers toward deeper understanding and realization.

The Nightingale's explanation of his love for the Rose and the Hoopoe's response offer a profound exploration of love, attachment, and spiritual pursuit. It's a dialogue that resonates with the universal human experience, reflecting the complexities of love, the challenges of transcendence, and the eternal quest for the divine. It serves as both a mirror and a guide, reflecting human vulnerabilities and illuminating the path toward true love and enlightenment. The lessons derived from this conversation continue to inspire and challenge readers, making it a timeless and deeply resonant part of Attar's masterpiece.

CHAPTER 3

Reflections of Desire: Unveiling Spiritual Truths in the Dialogue between the Parrot and the Hoopoe

The dialogue between the Parrot and the Hoopoe unfolds as a tapestry of profound allegorical revelations, inviting us to delve deeper into its layers of meaning. At its core, this exchange serves as a metaphor for the human condition, where our fixation on external appearances often blinds us to the deeper truths that underlie our existence.

The Parrot's initial refusal to embark on the quest is a reflection of his attachment to the superficial and the transient. His infatuation with the colorful reflection in the mirror mirrors our own human tendencies to be enamored with physical beauty, pleasure, and the fleeting joys of the material world. In this sense, the Parrot's obsession with his own reflection becomes emblematic of the broader human dilemma – our entanglement with form and our difficulty in seeing beyond mere appearances.

To the Parrot, the reflected image represents not just physical allure but also a divine manifestation, a gateway to the spiritual realm. He genuinely believes that his devotion to this image is a legitimate path to spiritual enlightenment. However, the Hoopoe, embodying wisdom and insight, sees through the Parrot's attachment to appearances.

The Hoopoe's response is multi-faceted. On one hand, it compassionately recognizes the Parrot's sincerity in his devotion but, on the other, it challenges the Parrot's fixation on the superficial. The Hoopoe's teachings revolve around the fleeting and impermanent nature of physical beauty. Through this enlightening exchange, the Hoopoe imparts the wisdom that beauty is, by its very nature, transient – like morning mist that dissipates as moments pass. The Parrot's attachment to this ephemeral beauty unwittingly ensnares him in a relentless cycle of desire and attachment. This cycle, driven by the pursuit of fleeting beauty, keeps the Parrot confined within the material realm, distancing him from the profound essence that lies beneath the surface of existence.

The Hoopoe's guidance is firmly grounded in the understanding that the allure of physical beauty is inherently ephemeral, subject to the ceaseless march of time. In this evanescent state, beauty is incapable of offering lasting fulfillment, for it dissolves like the morning mist. By clinging tightly to this illusory reflection, the Parrot unwittingly binds himself within a never-ending cycle of desire and attachment. This cycle, fueled by the pursuit of fleeting beauty, keeps the Parrot imprisoned within the confines of the material world, preventing him from recognizing the profound essence that underlies all of existence.

The Hoopoe's teachings reverberate as a timeless lesson in the impermanence of the material world. By illustrating the limitations of seeking fulfillment solely through the pursuit of physical beauty, the Hoopoe encourages the Parrot to transcend the allure of appearances and venture into a realm where true nourishment for the soul is found. Through his counsel, the Hoopoe prompts the Parrot to shift his focus from the ephemeral to the eternal, guiding him away from the confines of attachment and towards the boundless realm of spiritual liberation.

In this exchange, the Hoopoe masterfully exposes the paradox of attachment to impermanence. He offers the Parrot an opportunity to break free from the cycle and embark on a deeper, more meaningful journey towards truth. The Hoopoe contends that authentic beauty resides within the very core of all creation – a divine luminosity that transcends the limitations of materiality. This radiant spark, an embodiment of the sacred within everything, remains constant even as outward appearances change and fade.

The Hoopoe's wisdom draws attention to the fallacy of fixating on external allure, as it often blinds individuals to the more profound, enduring beauty that holds the potential to illuminate their spiritual path.

By cautioning the Parrot against becoming entrapped by the fleeting glamour of external appearances, the Hoopoe guides it towards a deeper realization. The Parrot's initial resistance mirrors the human inclination to be ensnared by the allure of surface beauty, causing one to neglect the transformative journey that leads to spiritual awakening.

The Hoopoe's counsel emphasizes that the true essence of enlightenment lies in recognizing and embracing the intrinsic divinity that resides within all aspects of existence. It invites us to transcend the limitations of appearances and connect with the enduring and profound beauty of the soul.

The Hoopoe's refutation is also an invitation to transcendence, a call to embark on the spiritual journey that leads beyond the boundaries of form, desire, and attachment. He invites the Parrot to let go of his fixation on the reflection and to seek the eternal, unchanging truth that lies beyond appearances.

By entreating the Parrot to release its preoccupation with mere reflections, the Hoopoe encourages a release from the chains of illusion that bind one's perception. This advice underscores the notion that true liberation arises when one can detach from the allure of external appearances and venture into the realm of profound understanding. The Hoopoe beckons the Parrot – and by extension, humanity – to disentangle from the ephemeral, recognizing that it is through this liberation that one can uncover the timeless veracity that remains unaltered amidst the ever-shifting tides of change.

The Hoopoe's plea for the Parrot to shift its focus from the transient to the eternal parallels the transformative stages of a spiritual journey. It's an invitation to shed the layers of attachment to the material world and embark upon a pilgrimage towards inner enlightenment. The Hoopoe's words remind us that the genuine essence of reality lies beyond the deceptive façade of appearances, and it's only through this shift in perspective that one can embrace the unchanging and universal truth that resides at the core of existence.

This narrative of transcendence and inner exploration is a testament to the Hoopoe's sagacity. By encouraging the Parrot to relinquish the superficial allure of reflections, the Hoopoe guides it towards the profound endeavor of discovering its own true nature, one that isn't bound by transient forms but is aligned with the eternal and boundless essence that transcends the physical world.

The Hoopoe's words echo as an invitation to embark upon a profound spiritual odyssey, beckoning the Parrot – and all who resonate with its journey – to journey beyond appearances and into the realm of the eternal. It's a summons to relinquish attachments, unravel desires, and pierce through the veil of illusion to uncover the unchanging truth that resides at the heart of all existence.

The Hoopoe's wisdom unveils the inherent barriers that clinging to superficial beauty erected on the path to inner awakening. Through this teaching, the Hoopoe emphasizes the necessity of transcending the allure of the physical realm in order to embark on a journey toward divine truth.

The Hoopoe's insights illuminate the truth that genuine spiritual progress necessitates a profound detachment from the material world. By focusing on the ephemeral, superficial aspects of existence, individuals tend to become ensnared in the web of desires and attachments. These attachments act as chains that bind and confine, preventing one from reaching the higher echelons of self-realization and divine understanding. The Hoopoe's counsel, therefore, serves as a gentle yet resolute call to release these shackles and embrace the path of liberation through non-attachment.

The Hoopoe's teachings mirror the profound wisdom found in various spiritual traditions, where non-attachment is deemed essential for genuine spiritual progress. By letting go of the fixation on surface beauty and material gains, individuals become capable of experiencing a higher state of consciousness and a deeper connection with the universal truth that permeates all existence.

Ultimately, the Hoopoe's discourse encapsulates the essence of spiritual growth as a journey toward detachment. It beckons individuals to release the grip on the fleeting and embrace the eternal. By navigating the realms of non-attachment, seekers can transcend the limitations of the material world and uncover the boundless, unchanging truth that resides within. The Hoopoe's counsel stands as a guiding light, inviting all to embark on this transformative expedition toward realizing the profound beauty of the soul and the interconnectedness of all things.

The wisdom of detachment is a central lesson, showing how attachment to the material world is a barrier to spiritual growth. The Hoopoe teaches that non-attachment is a pathway to liberation, enlightenment, and union with the Divine. The dialogue also underscores the essence of spiritual pursuit, the journey from attachment to liberation, from form to essence, from the reflection to the Source. It illustrates the transformative power of the spiritual path and invites readers to embark on their personal quests for divine truth.

CHAPTER 4

Unmasking Pride and Embracing Humility: The Dialogue Between the Peacock and the Hoopoe

The dialogue between the Peacock and the Hoopoe in "The Conference of the Birds" by Fariduddin Attar adds a layer of complexity and depth to the narrative, unveiling intricate facets of human nature and spirituality. This conversation serves as a powerful juxtaposition of contrasting themes, including worldly pride and humility, arrogance and wisdom, and the pursuit of superficial status versus the pursuit of true spiritual greatness.

The Peacock's decision to abstain from embarking on the journey to find the Simorgh provides a profound exploration of the pitfalls of pride and attachment to one's external appearance. With its resplendent and mesmerizing feathers, the Peacock symbolizes ostentation and the vanity that often accompanies it. Its outward beauty becomes a source of arrogance, leading it to believe that it already embodies a form of divine magnificence. This fixation on its own splendor blinds it to the essence of the spiritual journey, causing it to overlook the deeper layers of self-discovery and transformation that lie ahead.

The Peacock's argument that its beauty is indicative of God's favor illustrates how ego can manipulate even the most divine gifts into tools for self-aggrandizement. By using its appearance as a measure of spiritual attainment, the Peacock falls into the trap of equating external admiration with inner enlightenment. This line of thinking blinds it to the true nature of spiritual growth and blinds it to the need for humility, self-awareness, and the relinquishment of pride.

Furthermore, the Peacock's belief that it is already dwelling in a heavenly realm due to its beauty highlights the danger of complacency in one's spiritual journey. This perception serves as a cautionary tale about the ease with which individuals can become satisfied with their current state, stagnating in their growth and failing to recognize the vast potential that lies beyond their immediate perceptions.

The Peacock's stance resonates as a reflection of the human tendency to value materialistic achievements and external validation, often at the cost of true inner development. In contrast, the Hoopoe's role as a wise guide underscores the significance of humility, self-examination, and the pursuit of genuine spiritual understanding. Through the Peacock's character, Attar masterfully highlights the need to transcend the limitations of pride, relinquish attachments, and embrace the profound journey of self-discovery that leads to the Simorgh, the ultimate truth.

In this dialogue, Attar crafts a narrative that delves into the intricacies of human psychology and spirituality, painting a vivid picture of the challenges one must navigate on the path to enlightenment. Through the Peacock's perspective, readers are reminded of the dangers of allowing ego and pride to obstruct the pursuit of true inner greatness, while also highlighting the transformative power of humility and the quest for deeper understanding that the Hoopoe embodies.

The exchange between the Hoopoe and the Peacock encapsulates a profound discourse that resonates far beyond its allegorical context. The Hoopoe's response serves as a multi-faceted refutation, gently yet decisively unraveling the web of illusions spun by the Peacock's worldly pride and status.

At the heart of the Hoopoe's eloquent retort lies a challenge to the Peacock's attachment to superficial worldly status. The Hoopoe masterfully directs attention away from external appearances and the fickle admiration of others, emphasizing that the true essence of greatness surpasses the ephemeral nature of transient beauty. By drawing attention to the fleeting and impermanent nature of worldly status, the Hoopoe exposes the shallowness of the Peacock's pride and the emptiness of seeking validation from the external world.

The Hoopoe's wisdom extends even further, weaving a tapestry that highlights the distinction between the illusion of grandeur and the profound reality of humility, wisdom, and spiritual connection. He dismantles the Peacock's illusion of superiority by revealing the inherent limitations of pride and arrogance. The Hoopoe guides the Peacock to recognize that true strength lies not in asserting dominance but in acknowledging and embracing one's limitations. This pivotal realization opens the door to genuine growth and transformation, untethered from the constraints of ego-driven perceptions.

In a narrative marked by the theme of humility, the Hoopoe underscores its pivotal role in the journey toward spiritual greatness. The Hoopoe's instruction resonates as an invitation to unravel the layers of ego and false self-importance. By humbly stepping away from the pedestal of pride, individuals can delve into the realm of self-awareness, where wisdom and understanding blossom. The Hoopoe's teachings illuminate the transformative potential of humility, serving as a conduit for deep communion with the Divine – a concept that transcends the transient allure of materialistic pursuits.

Yet, the Hoopoe's response is not solely a dissection of the Peacock's flawed beliefs; it's an invitation to embark on a profound journey of self-discovery and spiritual awakening. Through his words, the Hoopoe extends a compassionate hand, inviting the Peacock – and indeed, all who resonate with its struggle – to relinquish the weight of pride and arrogance. The Hoopoe's invitation resonates as a call to venture beyond the boundaries of ego, towards the eternal truth that lies beyond appearances.

The Hoopoe's response is a multifaceted gem, revealing the transience of worldly pride, the potency of humility, and the transformative power of the spiritual journey. It offers not only a critique of ego-driven attachments but a roadmap to liberation, wisdom, and true greatness. This exchange serves as a timeless reflection of our own struggles and aspirations, echoing the timeless wisdom that remains relevant across cultures and epochs.

The exchange between the Peacock and the Hoopoe imparts invaluable insights to readers. Attar's allegorical conversation masterfully paints a panoramic portrayal of human nature and spiritual evolution. The Peacock's display of pride in its worldly status mirrors humanity's deep-rooted attachment to external validation, success, and appearances. It serves as a poignant reminder of how easily we can become ensnared in the pursuit of societal recognition, often conflating it with authentic greatness.

In response, the Hoopoe's words shed light on the essence of genuine greatness. He emphasizes that this greatness thrives in qualities such as humility, wisdom, and an unwavering connection with the Divine. This serves as a vital shift away from the narrow confines of physical beauty and societal status.

Moreover, the dialogue serves as a mirror to the illusory nature of superiority. Through the Peacock's narrative, Attar deftly exposes the detrimental impact of pride and arrogance on spiritual growth. The Hoopoe's teachings echo a profound truth: that real strength stems from acknowledging our limitations and seeking growth through humility and introspection.

Humility emerges as a central theme, representing a gateway to wisdom, understanding, and communion with the Divine. Contrary to misconceptions, the dialogue underscores that humility isn't a sign of weakness but a wellspring of strength, a pathway to genuine greatness.

The fleeting nature of worldly achievements takes center stage in the conversation, underscoring their impermanence and ultimate dissatisfaction. This reminder encourages readers to embark on a more profound quest for lasting fulfillment through spiritual exploration.

The dialogue acts as a vivid illustration of the transformative potency inherent in the spiritual journey. It traces a passage from pride to humility, from the illusion of worldly status to the revelation of eternal truth. Through this, readers are beckoned to embark on their unique path, guided by wisdom, humility, and the quest for the eternal.

The Peacock's pride-driven stance and the Hoopoe's sagacious response within "The Conference of the Birds" poignantly delve into the realms of human pride, arrogance, and the pursuit of authentic greatness. Attar's narrative artfully untangles the intricate threads of worldly success, appearance, and validation, steering readers toward profound and enduring truths. The lessons derived from this exchange echo universally, continuing to kindle inspiration and provocation. This dialogue stands as a timeless cornerstone of Attar's spiritual narrative, holding a mirror to our attachments, illusions, and latent potentials, all while illuminating the journey towards genuine fulfillment and a profound connection with the divine.

CHAPTER 5

Beyond Attachment: The Dialogue Between the Duck and the Hoopoe

As the birds each present their range of excuses, a particularly profound interaction emerges between the Duck and the Hoopoe. This dialogue intricately weaves together strands of spiritual enlightenment, the complexities of human feelings, and profound metaphysical insights. As these two characters engage, they offer readers a captivating exploration into the depths of the human soul and the quest for divine understanding.

Central to this exchange is the Duck's profound affinity for water. On one level, water symbolizes a vital spiritual element, signifying purity and cleansing. It often serves as a metaphor for the divine source of life and spiritual renewal. The Duck's attachment to water can thus be seen as an allegorical representation of the human connection to the divine, the source from which all life flows. However, the Duck's relationship with water also becomes a metaphorical excuse, reflecting a familiar human tendency. The Duck's attachment to the familiar comforts of its watery domain becomes a barrier to embarking on the challenging journey to seek the Simorgh. This duality of water as both a symbol of the divine and a distraction emphasizes the intricate interplay between spiritual aspirations and worldly attachments.

The dialogue between the Duck and the Hoopoe raises questions about the nature of attachments and their potential to hinder the pursuit of higher truths. It delves into the complexities of human emotions and motivations, illustrating how even something as innocent as a fondness for water can be used as an excuse to resist transformative journeys. This mirrors the ways in which humans often cling to comfort zones, whether physical or emotional, rather than embracing the discomfort and uncertainty of spiritual growth.

By exploring the Duck's perspective, Attar prompts readers to reflect on their own attachments and excuses, encouraging them to consider the balance between embracing the divine and overcoming the allure of the mundane. This dialogue underscores the universal human struggle between the call of the spiritual and the pull of the material world, offering readers a mirror through which to contemplate their own spiritual journeys.

In response to the Duck's attachment to water and the excuses it presents, the Hoopoe's reply unfolds as a reservoir of profound wisdom and spiritual insight. The Hoopoe's words carry weight, as they not only address the Duck's specific concerns but also extend to universal themes of divine love and the transformative journey of the soul.

The Hoopoe's response serves as a gentle yet powerful challenge to the Duck's assumptions. With each carefully chosen word, the Hoopoe dismantles the Duck's limited perspective, encouraging it to delve deeper into the realms of understanding that transcend the surface of things. By addressing the Duck's attachment to water as a constraining factor rather than a liberating one, the Hoopoe initiates a shift in the Duck's perception.

Central to the Hoopoe's teachings is the distinction between the Duck's love for water and the all-encompassing love that transcends the boundaries of form. The Hoopoe guides the Duck to recognize that its attachment is confined to the physical, preventing it from experiencing the boundless and infinite love that exists beyond appearances. This insight becomes a mirror through which the Duck can reflect on its own limitations and explore the potential for profound spiritual growth. Furthermore, the Hoopoe challenges the Duck's preconceived notions of love, guiding it to comprehend a love that reaches far beyond the visible. This love, the Hoopoe explains, is characterized by an intense yearning and an insatiable desire for divine connection. It propels the seeker beyond comfort zones, pushing them to surpass the barriers that restrict their journey towards unity with the Divine.

The Hoopoe's refutation serves as an invitation, inviting the Duck to embark on a transformative journey of self-discovery and spiritual enlightenment. The Duck is encouraged to relinquish its attachment to the familiar, to release the confines of its comfort zone, and to embrace the limitless love that exists beyond the grasp of material forms. The Hoopoe's guidance offers the Duck a roadmap towards a deeper understanding of its purpose and existence, promising fulfillment through a union with the Beloved.

In this exchange, the Hoopoe embodies the role of both mentor and motivator, gently guiding the Duck towards a new paradigm of spiritual understanding. Through this interaction, the reader witnesses the profound impact of wise guidance and the potential for transcendent growth that awaits those willing to embark on the transformative journey towards divine realization.

This exchange, thus, between the Duck and the Hoopoe holds within it a treasure trove of invaluable lessons. At its core, the Duck's unwavering attachment to water serves as a symbolic representation of a quintessential human trait: our tendency to become entangled with forms, symbols, and outward appearances. It mirrors how we often find ourselves drawn to the familiar, the comfortable, and the known, mistakenly perceiving these aspects as the ultimate realization we seek.

The Hoopoe's reply to the Duck's attachment becomes a beacon of wisdom, shedding light on the significance of transcending superficial symbols. The Hoopoe's words resonate with readers, urging them to look beyond mere representations and to embark on a quest for the essential truth that surpasses all forms and limitations. As this dialogue unfolds, it casts a radiant spotlight on the essence of true love for the Divine. This love, the Hoopoe imparts, is not passive but rather an ardent flame, fueled by longing and desire. It compels the seeker to surge beyond the confines of their own limitations, to scale the heights that surpass boundaries, and ultimately to merge with the very Source from which all emanates.

An integral theme interwoven into this conversation is the notion of departing from comfort zones along the spiritual expedition. The Hoopoe, like a compassionate guide, imparts the understanding that authentic spiritual growth mandates courage, effort, and a willingness to relinquish the familiar in favor of the unknown. In its entirety, this dialogue extends a profound invitation to readers, beckoning them toward a heightened awareness of divine love—an understanding that transcends attachments, symbols, and forms. It serves as an inspiration to embark on a journey that leads to boundless connections, far removed from mere appearances. It calls upon all seekers to commence a transformative voyage toward authentic fulfillment and a harmonious union with the divine essence.

This interplay between the Duck's attachment and the Hoopoe's response reverberates beyond its narrative confines. It ventures into the realm of universal human experiences, encapsulating intricate emotions, desires, and yearnings. The Duck's affection for water symbolizes both the limitations and potential inherent within our attachments. Meanwhile, the Hoopoe's sagacity becomes a radiant path, guiding us toward the realms of transcendence, realization, and divine communion.

Attar's profound understanding of human nature and spiritual reality is encapsulated within this dialogue, perpetuating its guidance, inspiration, and insight. It stands as an everlasting testament to the timeless themes of love and realization, providing an intricate roadmap for those who traverse the path of self-discovery and spiritual illumination.

CHAPTER 6

Unveiling the Illusion: The Owl's Treasure and the Path to Spiritual Awakening

Within Fariduddin Attar's timeless work, "The Conference of the Birds," a profound dialogue unfolds between the Owl and the Hoopoe, resonating with deep philosophical insights and spiritual illumination. This exchange explores human attachments, earthly desires, and the pursuit of spiritual enlightenment, offering an allegorical portrayal of the struggle to release material possessions and the wisdom required to attain higher realization.

At the heart of the dialogue is the Owl, whose duty as a guardian of an ancient treasure serves as a powerful metaphor for human attachment to material wealth. The Owl's role mirrors humanity's tendency to cling to possessions, viewing them as essential to their identity and security. This depiction highlights the challenges of materialism and encourages readers to examine their own relationship with worldly riches. The Owl's identity becomes intertwined with the treasure, symbolizing how individuals often define themselves by their possessions, hindering their spiritual growth.

The Owl's hesitation to relinquish its role mirrors humanity's reluctance to sever ties with material comforts, justifying their attachment to material possessions as essential elements of their identity. This rationalization reveals the complex psychology of attachment to wealth, which can hinder spiritual growth.

In contrast, the Hoopoe's response offers profound wisdom, guiding both the Owl and readers towards higher understanding. The Hoopoe's words reflect the impermanence of material possessions and earthly desires, encouraging a shift in focus toward enduring spiritual wealth.

The Hoopoe begins by revealing the transient nature of material wealth, emphasizing its susceptibility to the passage of time. This redirection of attention towards a treasure beyond decay—the spiritual riches within the Divine's embrace—dispels the fallacy of control over earthly possessions. The Hoopoe conveys that true mastery resides in the spiritual realm, transcending the constraints of the material world.

The crux of the Hoopoe's counsel lies in a journey towards self-discovery, urging the Owl to uncover its identity beyond material accumulation. This guidance encourages introspection, illuminating the path to understanding one's purpose and connecting with the profound essence of life's spirituality.

The dialogue further elucidates the importance of detachment, with the Hoopoe's wisdom emphasizing that genuine spiritual growth comes from relinquishing attachments and transcending the allure of material possessions. This wisdom extends beyond the Owl's predicament, inviting readers to reflect on their own attachments and desires, as well as the path to spiritual elevation. The Hoopoe extends an invitation to embark on a spiritual expedition to encounter the Simorgh, awakening from the slumber of material obsession and yearning for a deeper alignment with the Divine.

The Hoopoe's counsel not only offers guidance but also promises transformation. It provides a roadmap with insights into the challenges and triumphs of spiritual awakening, emphasizing the need for letting go of temporal treasures in favor of eternal ones such as love, wisdom, and the transcendence attained through spiritual realization.

In the intense debate between the Owl and the Hoopoe, readers witness the battle of attachment versus liberation, a struggle deeply embedded in the human experience. The Hoopoe's wisdom sheds light on the shadows of attachment, offering a compass for the spiritual journey. As the Owl grapples with its treasures, it becomes a reflection of our collective struggles, while the Hoopoe serves as a guide leading us toward spiritual fulfillment. In this interplay of avian voices, Attar's eternal narrative continues to resonate, guiding us through the inner labyrinth to discover the true treasures awaiting us beyond the ephemeral.

The Owl's narrative, coupled with the Hoopoe's insights, serves as an allegorical roadmap to awakening. This exchange underscores the importance of discernment, enabling us to differentiate between the fleeting allure of the material world and the enduring pursuit of spiritual advancement. Readers find themselves within a hall of mirrors, reflecting their own attachments and receiving guidance on navigating them. Attar's words transcend time, prompting readers to contemplate the age-old dilemma of materialism and the spiritual path. As the Owl navigates its treasures, the Hoopoe illuminates the path of enlightenment—a path that demands the shedding of earthly attachments in favor of transcendent treasures within the soul's realms.

CHAPTER 7

Transcending Earthly Bonds: The Dialogue Between the Falcon and the Hoopoe

Each bird embodies distinct symbolic representations of specific human archetypes or the various challenges encountered on the path to spiritual enlightenment. As the narrative unfolds, the dialogue between the Falcon and the Hoopoe takes center stage, delving deeply into themes of loyalty, duty, and the eternal struggle between earthly attachments and spiritual yearning.

The Falcon and the Hoopoe, through their dialogue, exemplify the convergence of multifaceted human qualities that often resonate with the human experience. The Falcon, symbolizing courage, strength, and the spirit of a warrior, engages in a dialogue that explores the essence of its own being. This majestic bird represents the quest for purpose and the unwavering determination to fulfill one's responsibilities. On the other side of this intricate exchange stands the Hoopoe, a wise and venerable figure embodying profound insight and spiritual guidance. Serving as a guide, the Hoopoe illuminates truths that transcend the material world.

As the Falcon and the Hoopoe engage, the narrative peels back the layers of loyalty and duty weighing on the Falcon's heart. These aspects, deeply ingrained in human nature, find allegorical resonance within the Falcon's character. The Falcon's struggles mirror the constant tension individuals face—the conflict between the demands of the earthly realm and the soaring aspirations of the spiritual heart. This duality between the material and the metaphysical weaves a narrative thread that resonates universally, inviting readers to reflect on their own aspirations and responsibilities.

The Falcon's decision to decline the journey to find the Simorgh stems from its unwavering loyalty to the earthly king. In this metaphorical context, the Falcon represents those devoted to worldly power, leadership, and governance. It takes pride in its royal connections and views its duty to the earthly king as noble and honorable. The Falcon sees its service to the king as the embodiment of its purpose and identity, a mission that gives meaning and direction to its life.

However, the Falcon's refusal also reveals a complex duality between earthly loyalty and divine aspiration. Its loyalty to the earthly king signifies an attachment to worldly power and prestige, but it also hints at a shadow of spiritual yearning. In serving the earthly king, the Falcon glimpses echoes of divine kingship and eternal sovereignty. Its loyalty to the earthly king serves as both a barrier to spiritual realization and a distorted reflection of its deeper longing for union with the Divine.

The Falcon's plight finds its counterpart in the Hoopoe's wisdom. The Hoopoe's counsel, while directed at the Falcon, encapsulates universal teachings mirrored in many spiritual traditions. It is a timeless narrative, highlighting the importance of maintaining detachment from the material world while remaining committed to worldly responsibilities. The Hoopoe's guidance illuminates the path to a harmonious equilibrium, offering insight into the journey that involves remaining grounded while reaching for spiritual heights.

In this dialogue, readers are drawn into a profound exploration of the human condition, where loyalty, duty, and spiritual aspiration intersect. Attar's words transcend the boundaries of time, speaking to the timeless struggles and aspirations of humanity. As readers navigate the intricacies of the Falcon's quest, they are guided by the Hoopoe's wisdom. This dialogue etches itself as an invaluable gem within the larger tapestry, resonating as a beacon of guidance, introspection, and inspiration for all seekers and individuals striving to harmonize their worldly commitments with their spiritual yearnings.

In response to the Falcon's internal dilemmas regarding loyalty, duty, and spiritual yearning, the Hoopoe crafts a response that is both intricate and profound. With the Falcon's concerns laid bare, the Hoopoe steps in with wisdom that dissects the Falcon's loyalty to the earthly king. The Hoopoe's words serve as a mirror, revealing the transient and impermanent nature of worldly powers. Like a seasoned philosopher, the Hoopoe reminds the Falcon that these kings and rulers, like all things in the material realm, are bound by the shackles of change, decay, and mortality. Through this perspective, the Hoopoe gently dismantles the illusions that veil the Falcon's perception. But the Hoopoe does not stop at deconstruction; it proceeds to build a foundation of loyalty that transcends the material. In the Hoopoe's teachings, the Falcon's loyalty is not confined to fleeting earthly dominions; rather, it should ascend to the eternal Divine King—the source of all sovereignty. The earthly king's allure becomes a mere shadow, a distorted reflection of the Falcon's inherent allegiance to the Creator. The Hoopoe beckons the Falcon to recognize the depth of this intrinsic loyalty, guiding it toward the realm where the heart's devotion and service flourish under the light of the Divine.

The Falcon's attachment to earthly accolades undergoes a similar unraveling. The Hoopoe's guidance pierces through the mirage of prestige, power, and honor, revealing them for what they are—transitory illusions that bind the soul to the realm of appearances. Instead, the Hoopoe illuminates the true hallmarks of honor, not etched in titles or temporal connections, but rather in humility, wisdom, and the relentless pursuit of spiritual enlightenment.

As the Falcon grapples with its dilemmas, the Hoopoe offers not just critique but a map toward the ultimate destination—divine union. In these words, the Falcon finds an invitation to loosen its grip on worldly attachments, to transcend the confines of its identity, and to embark on a journey of unfurling wings toward oneness with the Divine. The Hoopoe extends a hand of guidance and wisdom, serving as a compass through the labyrinth of human struggles, ultimately illuminating the path to true fulfillment and everlasting connection. The Falcon's inner turmoil becomes a canvas upon which the Hoopoe paints profound insights. The dialogue oscillates between the Falcon's doubts and the Hoopoe's responses, resulting in an exquisite mosaic that captures the essence of human dilemmas and spiritual yearnings. This exchange stands as a testament to Attar's profound understanding of human nature, serving as a timeless guide that offers solace, guidance, and a roadmap to those who traverse the intricate journey of self-discovery and spiritual enlightenment.

The interaction between the Falcon and the Hoopoe yields profound teachings, unfolding a masterful tapestry that resonates with resonant insights. Indeed, this dialogue transcends its avian characters to encapsulate the intricacies of human existence.

At its core, the Falcon's unwavering allegiance to the earthly king becomes a profound metaphor. This attachment mirrors the human penchant for pursuing power, prestige, and material connections. The Falcon represents the complexities woven into our worldly duties, honor-bound responsibilities, and the intricate web of identity within the earthly sphere.

In response, the Hoopoe emerges as a sage interlocutor, ushering forth revelations that radiate far beyond the confines of the Falcon's predicament. The Hoopoe's words lead the Falcon and readers alike along a path of enlightenment, revealing that genuine fulfillment and realization lie beyond the limits of earthly attachments. This wisdom serves as a lighthouse guiding us away from the treacherous shoals of transient loyalties, powers, and honors.

Crucially, the dialogue brings to the fore the essence of authentic loyalty—an allegiance not directed towards fleeting worldly dominions, but towards the eternal Divine King. The Falcon's struggle mirrors our own battles, and the Hoopoe's teachings resonate universally. This true loyalty springs forth as an embodiment of the soul's innate connection with its Creator, transcending all boundaries that earthly life imposes.

Unveiling the ephemeral nature of worldly prestige, power, and honor, the dialogue leads us into profound contemplation. The Hoopoe's guidance navigates us through the illusory maze of transient satisfactions, steering our focus towards the enduring virtues of humility, wisdom, and the pursuit of divine revelation.

More than a mere exchange, this dialogue illustrates the transformative power inherent within the spiritual expedition. It maps the passage from the confines of earthly loyalty to the expanse of divine unity. It encapsulates a journey that transcends narrow identities to fuse with an eternal connection—a testament to the transformative metamorphosis each soul can undergo.

Embedded within this dialogue is an invitation—a call to arms beckoning readers to traverse the terrain of spiritual growth, guided by the light of wisdom, the compass of humility, and the magnetic force of eternal longing.

The dialogue becomes a mirror reflecting our own human struggles, as the Falcon's quandary symbolizes both our limitations and our potentials. In turn, the Hoopoe's wisdom blazes a trail toward transcendence, realization, and connection with the divine. This conversation is Attar's gift to seekers, echoing across time as a profound testament to his profound comprehension of human nature and the essence of spirituality. It offers solace, insight, and guidance to all who venture upon the path of love, loyalty, and spiritual awakening—a timely reminder that the ephemeral attachments of the material realm can be transcended, allowing us to ascend toward the boundless love and wisdom that are intrinsic to our very being.

CHAPTER 8

Embracing the Abyss: The Dialogue Between the Heron and the Hoopoe

In the tapestry of Fariduddin Attar's timeless masterpiece, "The Conference of the Birds," a poignant and intricate conversation unfolds between the Heron and the Hoopoe. Within the confines of this dialogue lies a profound and multilayered exploration of fear, courage, uncertainty, and the yearning for spiritual ascent. This exchange acts as a portal, inviting readers to journey into the depths of human emotions and spiritual evolution. The Heron's apprehension, symbolic of our own hesitations and anxieties, becomes a focal point of reflection. It mirrors the innate human fear of the unknown and uncharted territories. Just as the Heron grapples with the immensity of the Sea's depths, humanity too faces the abyss of uncertainties that life presents. This confrontation with fear and the struggle to transcend it resonate universally, touching the core of our human psyche.

Beyond the Heron's personal hesitation lies a profound symbolism. The Sea, stretching infinitely before it, becomes a canvas upon which the vastness and mystery of divine reality are painted. The Heron's fear of the Sea's unfathomable depth mirrors humanity's fear of the vastness and enigma that shrouds existence. This fear of the infinite becomes emblematic of our struggle to comprehend the boundless expanse of the universe and the intricacies of the spiritual realm.

A layer deeper, the Heron's reluctance to dive into the Sea's abyss reveals a fear of self-dissolution. The Sea's depth becomes a metaphor for the dissolution of the ego—the obliteration of the known self in the boundless embrace of divine love. The Heron's hesitance to plunge into the depths of the Sea echoes humanity's fear of surrender—the fear of relinquishing control, of losing the familiar and comfortable identity that we cling to.

Central to the Heron's apprehension is the belief that the Sea's depth is insurmountable—a sentiment that strikes a universal chord. This justification reverberates with echoes of inadequacy, embodying the all-too-human notion that we are not strong enough, wise enough, or courageous enough to confront the vast mysteries of existence. The Heron's reasoning mirrors the human tendency to concoct rationalizations that anchor us in our comfort zones, preventing us from embracing risks, making transformative changes, and embarking on the path of spiritual growth.

Through the Heron's hesitation and the Hoopoe's guidance, readers find themselves at the crossroads of human vulnerability and spiritual potential. The dialogue transcends its avian characters, extending a compassionate invitation to confront our own fears, uncertainties, and limitations. The Heron's reluctance is a reflection of our collective hesitations, and the Hoopoe's counsel becomes a roadmap for traversing the sea of doubts, guided by the light of faith and courage. Just as the Heron's plight symbolizes the vast expanse of the Sea, so too does this exchange mirror the boundless journey of the human spirit—forging ahead into the depths of the unknown, propelled by the yearning for unity, enlightenment, and connection with the Divine.

The Hoopoe's response, like a beacon of wisdom, is a guiding light that pierces through the shroud of fear. The Hoopoe's words serve as a gentle yet powerful reminder that fear is a transient and fleeting emotion, while the essence of the Divine remains unchanging and eternal. This exchange unveils a profound insight into the interplay of fear and faith, elucidating how faith can act as a catalyst to dissolve the shackles of fear and uncertainty.

As the Hoopoe addresses the Heron's apprehensions, the reader is privy to a lesson in courage and spiritual aspiration. The Hoopoe invites the Heron to embrace the waves of the Sea with a heart imbued with trust and conviction. This call to overcome trepidation becomes a metaphor for the journey of self-discovery and spiritual evolution—each wave represents a challenge, an opportunity to conquer our innermost fears, and to dive into the depths of our being with faith as our guide.

The Hoopoe begins by challenging the Heron's fear, arguing that fear is a barrier, not a truth. He points out that fear is a creation of the mind, a limitation that prevents the soul from realizing its potential. The Hoopoe teaches that the fear of the unknown, the fear of losing control, and the fear of surrender are illusions that bind the soul to the material world. The Hoopoe also reframes the Heron's understanding of courage, teaching that true courage is not the absence of fear but the willingness to face it. He emphasizes that courage is the ability to step into the unknown, to take risks, and to embrace uncertainty. The Hoopoe calls the Heron to recognize its inherent courage, to overcome its fears, and to embark on the journey to divine realization.

The Hoopoe's refutation offers a pathway to surrender, a path that transcends fear and leads to union with the Divine. He invites the Heron to let go of its fears, to surrender its ego, and to plunge into the boundless ocean of divine love. The Hoopoe offers the wisdom that surrender is not a loss but a realization, a union with the eternal and infinite Source.

The Hoopoe also encourages the Heron to grow, to expand beyond its limitations, and to realize its potential. He emphasizes that growth requires risk, change, and the willingness to face uncertainty. The Hoopoe's encouragement is a call to spiritual growth, to the realization of the soul's innate wisdom, love, and potential.

This dialogue, while seemingly between two avian beings, uncovers the facets of the human experience. It reflects our collective yearning for growth, for courage in the face of adversity, and for the assurance that there's something beyond our immediate understanding. The Heron's reluctance is our own hesitation, and the Hoopoe's guidance serves as a mirror to the wisdom that exists within us. Through this dialogue, Attar delves into the human psyche, unraveling the complexities of fear and offering a pathway to transcendence, realization, and divine connection.

Through the Heron's uncertainty and the Hoopoe's counsel, readers are reminded that the path to spiritual ascent is akin to navigating the vast and unknown Sea of life. It is through courage, faith, and trust in the Divine that we can transcend our fears, allowing us to plunge into the depths of our inner selves and emerge transformed. The conversation serves as a guide and inspiration for all who seek to understand fear, cultivate courage, embrace surrender, and pursue the path of love, wisdom, and realization. It invites readers to plunge into the boundless ocean of divine love, to transcend fear, and to discover the infinite, eternal truth that lies within.

Attar's depiction of this exchange encapsulates not just the dynamics of a conversation but also the intricacies of the human journey. It stands as a testament to the author's deep understanding of the human psyche and the essence of spirituality. The dialogue resonates across time, inviting readers to embark on their own voyage, where fear is conquered by courage, uncertainty is embraced by faith, and the call of the spiritual realm is answered with a resounding yes.

CHAPTER 9

Guiding Light: Role of the Hoopoe as a Spiritual Guide

In the allegorical realm of Fariduddin Attar's "The Conference of the Birds," the character of the Hoopoe emerges as a multifaceted guide, embodying wisdom, compassion, patience, and strength, steering the birds on an intricate journey in search of the elusive Simorgh. As a central figure in this tale, the Hoopoe's role transcends the boundaries of fiction to reflect the profound qualities that guide souls through trials and tribulations. This narrative not only unveils the transformative odyssey of the birds but also casts light on the timeless significance of a spiritual guide, offering insights into the facets of leadership and guidance both within the context of the story and as a reflection of the roles guides play in our own lives.

In the grand theater of the birds' arduous journey toward the elusive Simorgh, the Hoopoe takes on the role of a radiant guiding presence, skillfully intertwining threads of wisdom, compassion, patience, and strength for every bird venturing forth on this transformative journey. The Hoopoe also takes center stage, its presence an embodiment of the profound qualities that steer souls through trials and tribulations. This allegorical tale not only offers a window into the birds' transformative voyage but also casts a spotlight on the timeless significance of a spiritual guide in the realms of both fiction and reality.

Within the heart of this narrative, the Hoopoe dons the mantle of leadership, becoming a steadfast beacon in the avian pilgrimage. With each flap of its wings and each word it imparts, the Hoopoe embodies wisdom—an ageless font from which the other birds drink, gleaning insights that illuminate the path of self-discovery. Its wisdom becomes the map that charts the uncharted territories of the spiritual journey, enabling the birds to traverse their personal and collective trials. The Hoopoe's profound wisdom is evident throughout the journey. It understands the nature of the path, the challenges to be faced, and the ultimate goal. It uses allegories, parables, and metaphors to convey profound truths and guide the birds to deeper understanding. This wisdom is reflective of the knowledge and insight that spiritual guides must possess to lead others toward enlightenment.

Compassion, a gentle current that runs through the Hoopoe's interactions, courses with a tenderness akin to the morning breeze. It understands the unique struggles and desires of each bird, guiding them with a gentle yet firm hand. This mirrors the essential quality of love and understanding that spiritual guides must exhibit to assist others on their path. This compassion becomes the balm that eases their weariness, fostering a sense of unity amidst diversity and reminding them that each has a place in the grand mosaic of existence.

Patience, a virtue as ancient as time itself, resides within the Hoopoe's presence. It acknowledges that growth unfurls at its own pace, like petals unfurling to meet the sun. The Hoopoe's unwavering patience becomes a mirror reflecting the cosmic patience of the universe, granting the birds the space and time to navigate their inner labyrinth and find their own unique song amidst the symphony of existence.

Strength, like the roots of an ancient tree, anchors the Hoopoe as it faces the storms and winds that assail the birds' resolve. It remains a pillar of resilience, unwavering in the face of doubts, fears, and setbacks. This strength becomes the birds' refuge, offering a sanctuary from the storms of uncertainty and a beacon of hope that illuminates the path ahead.

This allegorical tale, while seemingly nestled in the realms of fiction, resonates with profound truths that transcend the boundaries of the narrative. The Hoopoe's role mirrors the essence of spiritual guides in our lives—a compass that points toward self-discovery, a lamp that dispels the darkness of ignorance, and a steady hand that leads us through the labyrinth of challenges.

The Hoopoe leads the birds through seven treacherous valleys, each representing a stage in the spiritual journey. It understands the intricacies of the path and the transformations required at each stage, guiding the birds safely through. This role as a navigator symbolizes the spiritual guide's deep understanding of the spiritual path and the ability to guide others through its complexities. Throughout the journey, the Hoopoe both challenges and supports the birds. It pushes them to confront their deepest fears, illusions, and attachments, yet also offers support, encouragement, and wisdom. This dual role mirrors the delicate balance that spiritual guides must maintain between challenging and nurturing those they guide. The Hoopoe acts as a mirror, reflecting the birds' true nature back to themselves. Through its insights, the birds begin to see themselves more clearly and recognize their divine essence. This mirroring reflects the spiritual guide's ability to help others see their true selves, moving beyond ego and illusion.

The Hoopoe emphasizes the unity of all beings and the interconnectedness of all things. It teaches that the journey is not just individual but collective, leading to the realization of the oneness of all existence. This teaching mirrors the spiritual guide's role in helping others recognize the interconnectedness and unity of life.

As the birds soar toward the enigmatic Simorgh, we find ourselves soaring as well—toward a deeper understanding of the role a spiritual guide plays in our lives. Just as the Hoopoe guides the birds through their quest, so too do our own guides navigate us through the complex landscape of human existence. Attar's tale serves as a timeless reminder that amidst the complexities of our journey, the presence of a guide—a being embodying wisdom, compassion, patience, and strength—can illuminate the path, enabling us to transcend the ordinary and embrace the extraordinary in both our spiritual and everyday pursuits.

The Seven Valleys

CHAPTER 10

Embarking on the Spiritual Odyssey: Unveiling Wisdom of the Valley of Quest

With the Hoopoe's guidance echoing in their hearts, the assembly of birds stood at the edge of a vast expanse. Before them stretched a valley, known as the Valley of the Quest. Its landscape was both enchanting and daunting, with its rugged terrain and mysterious depths. The air was filled with a sense of anticipation as the birds prepared to take their first step into the unknown. As they entered the valley, the chirping and fluttering that once filled the air began to wane. The atmosphere grew hushed, and the birds' footfalls on the rocky ground seemed to echo the beating of their hearts. Each step they took carried the weight of their aspirations and fears, their hopes and doubts.

The Valley of the Quest was a place of introspection, a realm where the birds were forced to confront the doubts and uncertainties that had lingered in the shadows of their minds. It was a valley where the landscape mirrored the inner landscape of their souls. Yet, despite the challenges that lay ahead, a sense of unity and purpose prevailed among the birds. They walked side by side, supporting one another as they navigated the twists and turns of the path. The diversity of the assembly was transformed into a source of strength, as they shared stories, offered encouragement, and exchanged insights gained from their personal experiences.

As they journeyed deeper into the valley, they faced moments of doubt and confusion. Some birds faltered, questioning their decision to embark on this quest. The allure of the familiar and comfortable tugged at their wings, tempting them to turn back. But the memory of the Hoopoe's words and the vision of the Simorgh's radiant presence spurred them on. With each challenge they overcame, a new layer of understanding and determination unfolded within the hearts of the birds. The Valley of the Quest demanded that they confront their own limitations, transcend their doubts, and persevere despite uncertainty. This journey mirrored the inner struggle that seekers often encounter as they embark on a path of self-discovery and spiritual growth. As the birds traversed the valley, they realized that the journey was not just about reaching a destination—it was about the transformation that occurred along the way. Their initial desire to find the Simorgh had evolved into a deeper understanding of themselves and the nature of their quest. The valley had become a crucible for refining their intentions and deepening their commitment. And so, the birds continued to walk the path, guided by their collective longing and the lessons they had already learned. The Valley of the Quest had tested their resolve, and though their feathers might be ruffled by the challenges, their spirits remained unwavering. With each step, they moved closer to the realization that their journey was not only outward but also an exploration of their inner landscapes, a pilgrimage of the heart towards a truth that was both personal and universal.

The Valley of Quest, an enigmatic realm of yearning, doubt, and unity; a pivotal juncture that encapsulates the symbolism and esoteric beliefs guiding the journey of the birds toward self-discovery and union with the divine. The Valley, positioned towards the culmination of the birds' trials and tribulations, is a compelling metaphor that exemplifies the transformative power of challenges on an individual's beliefs, fostering spiritual growth and motivating them to embark on a profound spiritual expedition. The Valley serves as a microcosm of the spiritual path, embodying esoteric beliefs and symbolisms intrinsic to Sufism, a mystical branch of Islam that seeks direct experience of the divine. The valley is described as a desolate place, a barren expanse inhabited by venomous serpents and fearsome dragons, beset by treacherous precipices, and enshrouded in a perpetual mist. These features, while serving as physical obstacles, carry profound metaphorical meanings that are pivotal to the readers' understanding of the deeper spiritual themes of the narrative.

DESOLATION, DETACHMENT, AND SYMBOLISM OF CHALLENGES AND TRANSFORMATION

The barrenness of the Valley of the Quest serves as a symbolic representation of the challenges, doubts, and inner struggles that seekers encounter on their spiritual journeys. This barren landscape holds deeper meanings that reflect the transformative nature of the journey toward self-discovery and divine connection. It also symbolizes the inner emptiness and doubts that seekers often experience when they begin their spiritual journeys. Just as the valley lacks the lushness of growth and vibrancy, seekers may initially feel a void within themselves and question their readiness for the path ahead. This emptiness can arise from doubts about their abilities, the validity of their spiritual quest, or the path they've chosen. It signifies a stripping away of external distractions and attachments. In this desolate landscape, seekers are compelled to detach from the material world, shedding the superfluous and unnecessary aspects of their lives. This detachment is essential for cultivating an inner focus and a clearer perspective on what truly matters in their pursuit of divine truth.

The Valley of the Quest also presents challenges that test the resolve and commitment of the seekers. The difficult terrain, the absence of immediate rewards, and the uncertainty of the journey mirror the challenges that arise when individuals set out on a transformative path.

It prompts seekers to reflect on their motivations and strengthen their determination to continue despite hardships. The barrenness of the valley can symbolize confronting the ego or the lower self. Just as the landscape lacks external adornments, seekers must confront the illusions and attachments of the ego that often obscure their connection to the divine. The journey through this barren landscape involves battling the ego's resistance to change and growth. The lack of distraction encourages introspection and self-discovery. Seekers are compelled to turn inward and examine their inner landscapes. This inner exploration mirrors the process of self-discovery and self-awareness that is integral to the spiritual journey. The barrenness is not devoid of purpose—it prepares seekers for the transformations that will occur as they progress on their journey. The challenges of the valley shape their character, build resilience, and deepen their understanding of themselves and their relationship with the divine. As seekers navigate the barren landscape, they begin to see through the illusion of the material world's superficial allure. The valley's starkness encourages them to seek deeper truths beyond the surface, guiding them toward a more profound connection with the divine.

Ultimately, the barrenness of the Valley of the Quest serves as a metaphor for the necessary challenges and inner purification that seekers must undergo on their spiritual journey. It symbolizes the state of spiritual desolation, where the seeker has renounced the material world and embarked on a path of detachment. This spiritual detachment is fundamental in Sufism, as it signifies the process of letting go, confronting doubts, and transforming one's consciousness—a transformative passage that leads from spiritual desolation to a deeper connection with divine reality.

IMPACT ON INDIVIDUAL BELIEF AND MOTIVATION

The Valley of Quest's challenges have a profound impact on the birds' individual beliefs and motivations. The hardships they face strip away their superficial identities, forcing them to confront their true selves and prompting a reevaluation of their purpose. Each obstacle the birds overcome represents a significant shift in their perspective and belief system, gradually aligning them with the core tenets of Sufi mysticism. This phase of the allegorical journey serves as a crucible of transformation, challenging and shaping the birds' understanding, commitment, and resolve as they navigate it's barren landscape.

The challenges of the valley test the birds' belief in the quest and the guidance of the Hoopoe. The barrenness, hardships, and moments of doubt challenge the foundation of their belief. This testing, however, serves to strengthen their conviction and deepen their understanding of the journey's significance. The adversity they face allows them to move beyond superficial belief and cultivate a more profound and resilient faith.

As the birds navigate the valley's challenges, they undergo a transformative process that reshapes their beliefs. Initially motivated by curiosity, they soon realize that their individual desires and egos are inadequate for the journey. Through trials and hardships, their beliefs evolve from the desire for self-preservation to a deeper yearning for divine union and realization. As the birds navigate the difficulties of the valley, their initial motivations may shift and evolve. The allure of the Simorgh that first motivated them may be supplemented by a growing realization that the journey itself holds transformative power. The valley's challenges become an opportunity for inner growth and self-discovery. The initial external goal becomes intertwined with the internal realization that the journey is a path to deeper understanding and connection with the divine. It forces the birds to confront their inner struggles, doubts, and ego-driven resistances. This confrontation serves as a mirror, reflecting their inner complexities and the obstacles that hinder their spiritual progress. By facing these inner conflicts, the birds gradually gain insights into their own limitations and the need for inner purification.

Despite the hardships, the experience within the valley deepens the birds' determination to continue the journey. They realize that the pursuit of the Simorgh is not merely a matter of desire but a matter of commitment, perseverance, and surrender. The challenges encountered within the valley make them acutely aware of the need to transcend their comfort zones and continue despite difficulties.

The collective experience of the valley fosters a sense of unity among the birds. Sharing their struggles and supporting each other reinforces their motivation. The collective determination and mutual support create a sense of community that sustains their motivation even when faced with adversity. The barrenness of the valley serves as a canvas upon which the birds realize their inner transformation. The challenges they overcome and the doubts they confront lead to a gradual shedding of their ego-driven illusions. This realization of inner growth and transformation becomes a source of renewed motivation to continue the journey. The valley's challenges cultivate humility and surrender in the birds. The struggles they face expose their vulnerability and limitations, fostering a sense of humility and prompting them to submit to a higher power. This mirrors Sufi principles of acknowledging human frailty and recognizing the need for submission to the divine will.

The impact of the Valley of the Quest on individual belief and motivation is multi-faceted. It challenges and strengthens belief, shifts motivations from external goals to internal transformation, confronts inner struggles, deepens determination, fosters unity, and fosters a realization of inner growth. The experiences within the valley shape the birds' understanding of the spiritual journey's purpose, revealing that the emptiness holds not only challenges but also opportunities for profound inner change and a deeper connection with the divine.

The Valley encapsulates a treasure trove of esoteric beliefs and symbolic meanings central to Sufi mysticism. The valley's desolation, challenges, and transformative effects on the birds' beliefs exemplify the inner journey toward self-discovery and union with the divine. By navigating through treacherous terrains and battling inner demons, the birds undergo a spiritual metamorphosis that aligns them with the core values of Sufi philosophy. This allegorical narrative underscores the transformative power of challenges on individual beliefs and motivations, inspiring readers to embark on their own spiritual journeys toward self-realization and divine communion.

To the birds, the Hoopoe's words were a clarion call to a higher purpose, a quest that resonated with the human experience of seeking deeper truths and understanding. As Attar writes, "When they heard of the Simorgh's name, / Each bird was filled with hope and wonder. / Hope sprouted in their hearts, and wonder bloomed" (Attar, 101). This passage encapsulates the transformative moment when the birds' yearning was ignited, akin to the spark of inspiration that ignites the human pursuit of knowledge and meaning.

SYMBOLISM OF THE SIMORGH'S QUEST

The Valley of Quest unfolds as a pivotal juncture, where the universal pursuit of truth and purpose comes to the forefront. Essentially, this valley serves as a poignant allegory embodying humanity's profound yearning for truth and meaning. The birds' quest for the elusive Simorgh mirrors humanity's intrinsic drive to transcend the mundane and access profound knowledge. This pursuit symbolizes the universal human desire for self-discovery, connection, and spiritual enlightenment, forging an enduring link that surpasses historical and cultural boundaries. It stands as a reminder that the quest for truth is an inherently shared endeavor.

Within the Valley of Quest, the birds grapple with challenging terrain and a mist that symbolizes the veils of illusion and ignorance shrouding reality. Their progress unveils these layers of illusion, reflecting humanity's universal quest to perceive truths beyond superficial appearances. Serpents and dragons within the valley epitomize inner obstacles and ego-driven desires distorting reality. The birds' confrontation with these challenges mirrors the universal journey of self-discovery, where confronting inner struggles is essential for self-awareness and personal growth. Their collective resilience in facing the valley's trials underscores humanity's shared need for connection and cooperation. In a fragmented world, this allegory underscores unity and brotherhood as fundamental to the pursuit of truth, echoing humanity's yearning for a harmonious and interconnected existence.

The elusive Simorgh, the ultimate goal of the birds' quest, transcends mundane desires, reflecting humanity's inherent longing for something greater. This pursuit signifies the universal quest for higher purpose beyond fleeting gratifications. The birds' journey towards the Simorgh parallels humanity's journey towards self-realization and unity with the divine. It embodies the recognition that ultimate truth resides within, realized through inner transformation. Their quest mirrors the universal pursuit of divine knowledge and enlightenment, signifying an inner ascent towards spiritual awakening. This echoes humanity's collective aspiration to transcend limitations and attain higher knowledge, imbuing life with clarity, purpose, and fulfillment.

The culmination of their journey unveils that the Simorgh they sought reflects their own essence. This realization symbolizes the union between seeker and divinity, resonating with humanity's shared aspiration for connection with a higher reality and a profound sense of unity.

Navigating challenges and piercing illusions, the birds echo humanity's endeavor to transcend the ordinary, surmount inner barriers, and attain profound insights. The Simorgh's symbolism encapsulates humanity's intrinsic thirst for self-discovery, unity, and divine connection. Across cultures and epochs, this allegory reverberates, reminding us of our shared voyage towards understanding, self-realization, and the pursuit of truths beyond the mundane.

YEARNING AS THE CATALYST FOR GROWTH

The intense yearning that envelops the birds in their quest mirrors the profound emotion of longing that resonates within the human experience. This yearning, a fervent desire that transcends mere want, stands as a powerful catalyst capable of propelling individuals into the depths of self-discovery and a heightened perception of the world that envelops them.

As the birds embark on their journey through the valley, the very fabric of their narrative underscores the remarkable potential inherent in this yearning. It paints a vivid portrait of yearning's transformative nature, portraying it as a driving force that underpins the intricate mechanisms of personal and spiritual growth. In the narrative of the valley, yearning emerges as the compass that steers the birds towards a greater understanding of their own essence and their place in the intricate tapestry of existence. It calls them forward, urging them to confront their fears and uncertainties, and venture into the unknown with unwavering determination. Through this arduous yet enlightening journey, yearning becomes the fuel that propels them beyond their limitations, inviting them to explore the uncharted territories of their own potential.

The valley's narrative reflects how yearning can lead to self-discovery by compelling individuals to introspect, question, and ultimately transcend their perceived boundaries. It illuminates how yearning acts as a mirror, revealing the depths of one's desires, aspirations, and even insecurities. This introspective process, though challenging, is a pivotal step toward self-awareness and growth. Moreover, the narrative of the valley illustrates the capacity of yearning to kindle the flame of spiritual evolution. As the birds progress along their journey, their yearning evolves into a yearning for unity — a profound connection with the Simorgh. This transformation signifies a shift from personal desires to a desire for a greater, unified understanding of existence. Yearning, in this context, becomes a bridge between the individual and the divine, a force that drives them towards a heightened state of consciousness and a deepening communion with the spiritual realm.

The narrative of the valley showcases yearning's remarkable power to propel individuals beyond their comfort zones, to inspire profound introspection, and to catalyze a journey towards unity and enlightenment. It emphasizes that yearning is not merely a fleeting emotion, but a potent force that can reshape the trajectory of one's life, leading to a more profound understanding of oneself, others, and the universe at large.

CONFRONTING DOUBT AND SKEPTICISM

As the birds embark on their journey through the sprawling expanse of the valley, a new set of challenges comes into view. Among these challenges, doubt and skepticism rise to the surface like ripples in a tranquil pond. These moments of uncertainty, where shadows of hesitation dance across the path, serve as profound metaphors for the doubts that invariably accompany the pursuit of truth and higher understanding.

In the intricate narrative of the valley, doubt is not portrayed as a mere adversary to be shunned, but rather as an integral part of the seeker's path. It mirrors the wavering thoughts that often linger at the fringes of one's mind when venturing into the realm of the unknown. These moments of doubt are akin to uncharted territories, where questions arise, assumptions are challenged, and the very foundation of one's beliefs trembles.

Yet, the valley's story does not merely paint doubt as an obstacle; it also highlights the potential for growth and transformation that lies within it. These instances of uncertainty become signposts, guiding seekers toward an essential act of self-inquiry. In the face of doubt, the narrative suggests that it's not only permissible but also necessary to engage in introspection, to question the very fabric of one's beliefs, and to seek a deeper understanding of the truths being pursued.

Through this courageous process of self-inquiry, doubt undergoes a metamorphosis. It transforms from a barrier into a stepping stone. As the birds grapple with their uncertainties and engage in a process of soul-searching, they find that doubt, rather than hindering their progress, actually paves the way for a firmer foundation of faith and conviction.

In the broader context of the human journey, the narrative of the valley encourages seekers to confront doubt head-on, to embrace it as an opportunity for growth, and to allow it to refine their understanding. Just as a blacksmith tempers metal through fire, doubt tempers the seeker's convictions. By acknowledging doubt, seeking answers, and engaging in a deeper exploration of the self and the world, individuals can emerge from these moments with a more resilient faith—a faith not rooted in ignorance, but one that has weathered the storms of uncertainty.

In this way, the valley's narrative weaves doubt into the very fabric of the seeker's path, reminding us that the pursuit of truth is not a linear journey devoid of obstacles. Instead, it is a transformative odyssey where doubt serves as a catalyst for growth, enabling seekers to rise with greater clarity, confidence, and unwavering conviction in the truths they ultimately uncover.

DETACHMENT FROM WORLDLY DISTRACTIONS

During their expedition through vast landscapes, the birds find themselves confronted by a series of tempting distractions, each poised to lure them away from their ultimate goal: the quest for the Simorgh. These distractions, as they arise, unveil themselves as potent symbols of attachments, desires, and the seductive pull of the material realm. In the intricate narrative of the valley, these diversions become metaphors that shed light on the universal human inclination to be drawn off course by the ephemeral charms of the world.

In the vivid storytelling of the valley's narrative, these distractions hold a mirror to the attachments that often weigh down the human spirit. Just as the birds are enticed by these fleeting allurements, individuals can become ensnared by their own desires—yearnings for material possessions, worldly success, or sensory pleasures. The narrative serves as a reminder that these attachments, however captivating, can lead one astray from the deeper purpose of self-discovery and spiritual connection. Yet, the lessons of the valley do not conclude with the portrayal of these distractions as insurmountable obstacles. Instead, they unveil a profound teaching: the importance of detachment. Detachment here is not a renunciation of life's pleasures, but a conscious and intentional process of releasing the grip of worldly entanglements. By relinquishing attachments, individuals can create a sacred space within themselves—a space primed for inner exploration, reflection, and connection with the divine.

The valley's narrative urges seekers to navigate the labyrinth of desires with discernment, recognizing that true fulfillment lies not in the pursuit of transient pleasures, but in the unearthing of enduring truths. By loosening the hold of worldly cravings, individuals can elevate their consciousness, allowing the whispers of the soul to be heard above the cacophony of distractions. The essence of the valley's teachings is encapsulated in this process of detachment—a shedding of the unnecessary to make room for the profound. It is an invitation to prioritize the quest for inner wisdom over the fleeting glamour of the external world. Through detachment, individuals can liberate themselves from the chains of illusion and discover a more authentic connection with their own essence and the divine.

The valley's narrative, hence, serves as a reminder that the journey toward self-discovery and spiritual insight demands a conscious choice: the choice to let go of attachments that hinder growth and to create a space within where the authentic self can flourish. It's a lesson that resonates through time, guiding seekers towards a state of greater freedom, clarity, and communion with the divine.

HARMONY IN DIVERSITY: THE UNIFYING QUEST FOR TRUTH AND GROWTH

The assembly of birds, each representing a unique species and disposition, serves as a vivid embodiment of a profound theme: unity that rises above the surface of differences. As these avian individuals convene with a shared purpose—the pursuit of the elusive Simorgh—their collective endeavor transforms into a potent bond that surpasses their apparent disparities. This unified aspiration magnificently mirrors the collective endeavor of humanity, as individuals seek truth and traverse the path of spiritual enrichment together.

Embedded within the narrative of the valley is an invitation to comprehend the essence of unity that resides within diversity. The assembly of birds portrays a microcosm of the broader human experience—an amalgamation of cultures, backgrounds, and perspectives. Despite these disparities, the shared yearning for the Simorgh weaves an unbreakable thread of connection, demonstrating the universality of the human quest for understanding and higher meaning.

The valley's portrayal of unity goes beyond a mere notion of coexistence; it extends to a call for mutual support and shared growth. Just as the birds draw strength from one another to face the challenges of their journey, so too can humanity find strength in unity as they confront the enigmas of life and spirituality. The birds' collective endeavor becomes an allegory for the shared journey of humanity, one that traverses the landscapes of wisdom, growth, and enlightenment.

This resonant theme finds its eloquent expression in Attar's poetic verse: "Unity is life's essential state. / Where can this unity be found? / You will see it in the drop of rain." In these lines, the essence of unity unfurls as a fundamental principle woven into the fabric of existence. Just as a drop of rain dissolves into the vast ocean, so do the individual pursuits of seekers coalesce into a harmonious symphony of collective aspiration.

The valley's narrative underscores the interconnectedness that reverberates through the cosmos. It beckons individuals to recognize the shared journey they embark upon—a journey where personal enlightenment is interwoven with the growth of others. As the birds in the story find unity amidst diversity, so too can humanity forge a bond that transcends the confines of individuality. This unity in purpose and shared aspirations stands as a guiding star, illuminating the path to deeper understanding, spiritual enrichment, and a profound sense of oneness with all beings.

LESSONS LEARNED

The Valley of Quest imparts profound lessons and insights that serve as guiding lights for seekers on their personal quests for self-discovery:

Fulfilling the Soul's Yearning

Within the expanse of the valley, a profound illumination emerges—one that reveals the transformative power harbored within the realm of intense yearning. This yearning, a fire that burns within the human heart, possesses the ability to ignite an extraordinary inner journey when harnessed with purpose and intent. The narrative of the valley artfully presents this yearning as a gateway to uncharted territories of the self, a passage through which individuals can embark on a pilgrimage of self-discovery and spiritual awakening.

As the birds traverse the landscape, their yearning for the Simorgh serves as more than a simple desire; it becomes a vessel through which they sail the currents of their own souls. This yearning acts as a beacon, guiding them to delve deeper into the chambers of their inner world, urging them to unveil the hidden layers of their being. The valley's narrative encapsulates this process—a poignant reminder that yearning, when directed towards higher truths, is an initiatory force capable of propelling individuals into the depths of their own existence.

The valley's narrative unearths a hidden truth: the profundity of one's yearning corresponds to the profundity of their spiritual journey. Just as the birds' unwavering yearning for the Simorgh guides them through the landscape's challenges, so too can an individual's fervent yearning guide them through the complexities of their own inner landscape. The depth of yearning, like a compass, points the way towards the profound insights, revelations, and revelations awaiting discovery.

The narrative of the valley champions the notion that yearning is not to be suppressed or dismissed as mere emotion; rather, it is a precious resource to be acknowledged, cultivated, and embraced. It underscores the inherent significance of nurturing this yearning, tending to it as one would a fragile flame. In this nurturing, individuals kindle a flame that illuminates the path to self-awareness, spiritual growth, and an intimate connection with the higher realms of existence.

The valley's narrative invites individuals to view yearning not merely as a fleeting sentiment, but as a guiding force, a powerful catalyst that can transform the ordinary into the extraordinary. Just as the birds' yearning for the Simorgh propels them forward, so too can the yearning for truth and enlightenment lead individuals to a richer understanding of themselves and the universe. The valley's teachings resonate as a reminder that this yearning is not a mere facet of the human experience; it is a key that unlocks the door to the profound depths of the soul and the boundless expanses of spiritual growth.

Embracing Doubt

In the narrative of the valley, doubt takes on a transformative role, shifting its perception from being a mere stumbling block to an essential and inevitable aspect of the human journey. The journey through the valley is laden with moments of uncertainty and questioning, which, rather than impeding progress, becomes integral to personal and spiritual development.

The birds through this valley encounter doubt in their flight, much like how individuals encounter moments of skepticism and uncertainty on their life paths. These encounters, initially seen as challenges, are then revealed as profound opportunities for introspection and growth. As the birds are forced to pause in the face of doubt, they embark on a journey within themselves, questioning their beliefs, motivations, and perceptions.

Instead of shying away from doubt or hastily seeking easy answers, the seekers in this narrative choose a path of sincere inquiry and a quest for understanding. This deliberate approach allows them to peel back the layers of uncertainty and delve into the underlying causes of their doubts. They engage in a process of self-examination, critically evaluating their assumptions and confronting their deepest fears. This introspection not only clarifies their own convictions but also highlights the nuances of the broader world around them. Through this process, the doubt ceases to be a hindrance and evolves into a catalyst for growth. The seekers, having engaged with doubt thoughtfully and courageously, emerge with a stronger foundation upon which to build their faith. The understanding they glean from their journey enables them to transcend the limitations of uncertainty and skepticism. Their faith, now deeply rooted in personal reflection and genuine comprehension, becomes more resilient, capable of withstanding the storms of doubt that may arise in the future.

Ultimately, the valley's narrative teaches us that doubt is not an adversary to be feared, but a companion to be embraced. It reminds us that the human journey is marked by moments of uncertainty, and it is through these very moments that we have the chance to refine our beliefs, deepen our understanding, and strengthen our faith. By approaching doubt with an open heart and an inquisitive mind, we embark on a transformative voyage of self-discovery, leading us to a profound and unwavering connection with our convictions and the world around us.

Transcending Worldly Attachments

In the portrayal of distractions within the context of the valley's narrative, a poignant lesson unfolds—one that underscores the vital significance of detachment. This concept, encapsulated by the birds' transformative journey, highlights the deliberate act of relinquishing worldly diversions and cravings. Through detachment, individuals liberate themselves from the intricate web of material attachments, granting them the space and clarity needed to embark on a journey of inner reflection, self-discovery, and an enhanced communion with the divine.

The birds' expedition through the valley mirrors the human experience, where distractions in various forms tend to sway one's attention away from what truly matters. Yet, the narrative gently guides us to the realization that detachment is not a relinquishment of enjoyment or a rejection of the world's offerings, but rather a purposeful liberation from the chains of overindulgence. By willingly releasing our grip on the transient allure of material possessions and ephemeral desires, we create room for more profound explorations.

Detachment allows individuals to reorient their focus inward, to delve into the vast landscapes of their thoughts, emotions, and aspirations. Freed from the clamor of external diversions, seekers can engage in a process of introspection that unearths hidden motivations, unexamined beliefs, and untapped potentials. This journey of self-discovery becomes a transformative odyssey—a chance to discover the facets of one's identity that might have remained obscured amidst the cacophony of distractions.

Moreover, detachment provides a clearer channel for connecting with the divine or the spiritual essence that underpins existence. When unburdened by the constant pull of worldly concerns, individuals can attune themselves to a higher understanding, transcending the limitations of the material realm. This communion becomes more authentic, unmarred by the static interference of fleeting desires, allowing for a deeper, more meaningful connection with something larger than oneself.

In embracing detachment, one does not turn their back on the world, but rather steps back momentarily to gain a new perspective. It is a conscious choice to disentangle from the mundane in order to dive into the profound. By letting go of the trivial, individuals discover an unparalleled freedom—the freedom to journey within, to confront the depths of their being, and to soar to new heights of spiritual awareness.

The valley's narrative serves as a reminder that, in a world brimming with distractions, the art of detachment is a transformative power that nurtures the soul. By peeling away the layers of materialism and allowing the heart and mind to breathe, individuals can rekindle their connection with their true selves and the divine, ultimately leading to a life infused with purpose, authenticity, and a profound sense of fulfillment.

Unity in the Quest for Truth

Within the canvas of the valley's narrative, a striking testament to the potential of human unity emerges through the harmonious flight of the diverse birds. These avian travelers, hailing from distinct backgrounds and origins, unite in a compelling display of solidarity—a poignant reflection of the collective human pursuit of transcendent truths. This portrayal of unity, woven intricately into the story's fabric, resonates as a transcendent melody that rises above the cacophony of cultural, societal, and individual disparities.

The birds' convergence transcends the boundaries that often divide us, illustrating the universality of the human experience in the search for higher meaning. While their plumage might be a tapestry of differences, their shared flight signifies a shared purpose—an innate yearning to explore the mysteries of existence. It serves as a poignant reminder that beneath the surface, beyond the superficial divisions that fragment society, lies an intrinsic bond that unites us all as seekers of truth.

In an era marked by fractures and schisms, the narrative of unity in the valley becomes a beacon of hope, urging us to move beyond the confines of our differences and partake in a collective journey towards enlightenment. The message transcends mere coexistence; it invites us to intertwine our stories, our strengths, and our wisdom to create a tapestry that weaves together the myriad threads of human experience.

At its core, this portrayal of unity echoes the age-old wisdom that every individual is a note within the symphony of humanity. Each distinct note contributes to the symphony's richness, and it's only through harmonious collaboration that the melody of collective progress can be realized. The valley's narrative beckons us to recognize our interconnectedness, urging us to listen to the melodies of others, harmonizing our efforts and insights to create a harmonious resonance that resonates across cultures, eras, and souls.

In embracing this call to unity, we embark on a transformative journey—one that prompts us to shed the armor of bias and prejudice and instead embrace the vulnerabilities that come with openness. It compels us to engage in meaningful dialogues, to exchange perspectives, and to learn from one another's journeys. By transcending our individual narratives, we become part of a tapestry that tells the story of humanity's quest for enlightenment—a story that is richer, more vibrant, and more profound when united.

Ultimately, the valley's portrayal of unity transcends the confines of its narrative and emerges as an aspiration for our own lives. It encourages us to step beyond our comfort zones, celebrate our shared humanity, and embark on a collective pilgrimage towards higher truths. It's an invitation to harmonize our differences, to embrace our interconnectedness, and to contribute to a symphony of understanding that reverberates through time, reminding us that our shared endeavor is what truly unites us in our journey of seeking truth.

Embracing the Transformative Journey

Nestled within the heart of the Valley of Quest lies a revelation of immense significance: the journey itself, with all its twists and turns, is a crucible of transformation. The challenges, trials, and even the moments of disconcerting uncertainty that are woven into the path hold a hidden power—a power to shape, evolve, and illuminate. It is through these very trials that the seekers unearth the gems of personal growth, attain glimpses of profound insight, and nurture a more intimate understanding of both themselves and the intricate tapestry of the world around them.

The valley's narrative masterfully weaves the threads of experience, illustrating that each step taken along the path is a brushstroke upon the canvas of the self. The trials and tribulations encountered on the journey are not obstacles to be overcome, but rather catalysts for growth, akin to the sculptor's chisel that refines the raw material into a masterpiece. It is amidst the tempests of challenge that the seekers discover hidden reservoirs of strength within themselves, wellsprings of resilience they might never have known existed without the trials to draw them forth. Uncertainty, a shadow that often shrouds the path, emerges as a beacon guiding the seekers towards self-discovery. The moments of doubt and confusion, far from being detours, become crossroads that demand a deeper exploration of the self and the beliefs held. These are the moments when the seekers navigate the labyrinth of their own minds, confronting the limiting beliefs and assumptions that have held them captive. As they emerge from these encounters, they are reborn with a clearer vision of their path and a more profound connection to their inner compass.

Crucially, the valley's narrative underlines that every step upon the spiritual path brings the seekers closer to the realization of self and a profound union with the divine. Each footfall, no matter how faltering, is a stride towards self-actualization. Through introspection and the confrontation of challenges, the seekers peel back the layers of their being, shedding the masks they might have worn in the world and discovering the essence that lies beneath. With each step, they come to realize that the journey isn't a linear trajectory towards an external destination; it's an inward voyage that eventually leads them to the sanctum of their own souls. As the seekers inch closer to the summit of their quest, they find that the distance between themselves and the divine is narrowing. The realization dawns that the divine isn't some distant entity, but an integral part of their being. The journey itself becomes a dance of rediscovery—a rediscovery of their innate connection to the cosmos, their oneness with all of existence.

The Valley of Quest whispers an age-old truth: the journey isn't merely a means to an end—it is the very essence of transformation. The challenges that punctuate the path are the alchemical crucibles that transmute the ordinary into the extraordinary. The seekers, having traversed this transformative terrain, emerge not only with a deeper understanding of the world but, more importantly, with a profound awareness of themselves. The journey, with all its trials, tribulations, and revelations, is the vessel that carries them to the shores of self-realization and a harmonious union with the divine.

CONCLUSION

The Valley of Quest beckons to us like an ancient gateway, an entryway into a profound narrative that transcends the limitations of time and space. Its tapestry weaves together the threads of yearning, doubt, and unity, creating a rich tableau that resonates with seekers across generations. Unfurling without a discernible beginning or end, the valley becomes a metaphor for the perpetual journey of the human spirit—a journey that navigates the intricacies of existence, seeking enlightenment amidst the myriad twists and turns.

As seekers step into the embrace of this metaphorical valley, they encounter the palpable pulse of yearning—a force that stirs within the soul, a relentless call to explore beyond the confines of the ordinary. The valley illustrates that yearning is not mere restlessness, but a transformative energy that propels individuals to embark on quests of both the outer and inner realms. It is the driving force that urges seekers to traverse the arduous terrains of their own beings, unearthing the latent truths and dormant potentials that lie within.

In this sacred space, doubt is not a barrier but an integral part of the journey. The valley showcases doubt not as a weakness, but as a catalyst for introspection and growth. Like a crucible, doubt tests the resolve of seekers, prompting them to question the foundations of their beliefs and to confront uncertainty head-on. Through this confrontation, doubt becomes a stepping stone rather than a stumbling block, leading seekers to a deeper understanding and more resilient faith.

The valley's narrative unfurls with a serpentine grace, mirroring the labyrinthine passages of both the human psyche and the world's mysteries. In the midst of this labyrinth, the concept of detachment emerges as a guiding light. Seekers are urged to release their grasp on the ephemeral and the transient, embracing a state of detachment that enables them to gaze upon reality with clarity. It is through this detachment that they attain the ability to distinguish between illusion and truth, to perceive the essence beneath the surface, and to experience a newfound freedom from the entanglements of material desires.

Attar, the storyteller of this mystical realm, extends an enduring invitation—a beckoning call to humanity to partake in this sacred exploration. The Valley of Quest is more than a mere narrative; it is an invitation to engage in a profound odyssey of self-discovery and spiritual awakening. It prompts us to venture beyond the mundane, to dance with the forces of yearning, doubt, and unity, and to emerge on the other side with a deeper comprehension of our own essence and the interconnected tapestry of existence.

In the whispers of the valley's winds, we hear a timeless message—an invitation to embrace the journey, to be open to the transformative energies that course through our lives, and to recognize that every step taken is a step closer to profound self-realization and a harmonious union with the divine. The Valley of Quest, with its intricate narrative, serves as a perennial guide—a compass pointing us towards a deeper understanding of the self, the world, and the eternal quest for ultimate truth.

CHAPTER 11

Transcending Boundaries: An In-Depth Exploration of the Valley of Love

As the birds enter the Valley of Love, they are immediately enveloped by a sense of enchantment and the feeling of being drawn into a deeper realm of emotions. In this valley, they encounter a new set of challenges and experiences that will test their understanding of love and devotion. The valley serves as a place where love is explored in its various forms, including earthly, spiritual, and divine. The birds encounter manifestations of love that reflect different aspects of their own hearts and desires. As they journey through this valley, they witness the complexities and nuances of love, experiencing both its joys and its pains.

One of the first stories they encounter is that of Layla and Majnun, a tale of earthly love that highlights the intensity and longing that love can bring. Through this story, they begin to understand how love can consume one's heart and lead to both ecstasy and suffering. This narrative serves as a mirror for the birds to reflect on their own attachments and desires.

As the birds continue their journey through the Valley of Love, they also encounter stories of divine and spiritual love. They learn about the love of the Sufi mystics for the Divine Beloved and how their yearning for union with God drives them to renounce worldly attachments. These stories illuminate the theme of love as a path to spiritual enlightenment, leading the birds to reflect on their own yearning for the Simorgh.

Throughout the valley, the birds grapple with the complexities of love, understanding that it can be both an intoxicating force and a source of deep wisdom. They come to realize that love is not just an emotion but a transformative power that can lead to selflessness, unity, and a deeper connection with the divine. The Valley of Love serves as a crucial juncture in the birds' journey, where they confront the different facets of love and its role in their quest for the Simorgh. This chapter explores the theme of love as a driving force that compels seekers to transcend their individual desires and attachments, leading them closer to the realization of divine truth and unity. As the birds progress through the Valley of Love, they continue to evolve in their understanding of themselves and their purpose. This exploration sets the stage for further exploration of the birds' inner landscapes and their ongoing quest for spiritual realization.

"The Conference of the Birds" provides a profound and multilayered stage of the mystical journey that offers insight into the nature of divine and earthly love. The journey through this valley embodies the essence of Sufi teachings, providing a unique and complex exploration of love that can be interpreted in various ways. The Valley lies in a realm of significance that beckons the reader to embark on a transformative exploration of the multifaceted nature of love itself.

Attar's visionary perspective positions love as the very essence that propels the seeker's expedition toward union with the divine. The Valley serves as a reflective mirror, wherein the seeker beholds both the radiant allure and the challenging trials that love unfailingly bestows. Far from being confined to mere romantic or interpersonal connotations, the Valley of Love encompasses the full spectrum of love's manifestations: an ardor for the divine, a tender affinity for fellow beings, and an encompassing fondness for the world in all its intricacies.

As the birds travel along this valley, their experiences mirror those of the reader, compelling both to discern the myriad facets of love that course through their lives. Yet, this valley is not a serene meadow but a crucible of trials that demand profound introspection and transformation. Love, in Attar's vision, is both a catalyst for metamorphosis and a crucible that requires detachment and surrender. It is a transformative force that calls upon the seeker to relinquish the confines of the ego and, through selfless sacrifice, attain a heightened state of being.

Amid the enchanting expanse of Attar's Valley of Love, an intense transformation beckons the seeker, urging them to ascend beyond the shallowness of fleeting emotions and embark upon a journey into the depths of profound understanding. It is a realm where the heart's transient yearnings, like the ephemeral whispers of a passing breeze, encounter a resounding call—an invitation to embrace an enduring, eternal form of love that transcends the boundaries of time.

In this valley, the very essence of love becomes a luminous guide, illuminating the path towards a deeper connection with both the divine and the universe itself. The birds, symbolic pilgrims of the soul, and the readers who follow their flight, find themselves at a crossroads where the temporal and the timeless converge. They are invited to relinquish their attachments to transient desires and transient emotions, and to unveil the majestic tapestry of a love that resonates with the eternal rhythm of existence.

Contemplation becomes the lantern that lights this path. The seeker, much like the birds, is encouraged to turn their gaze inward, exploring the intricacies of their own hearts. Through introspection, they come to realize that the superficial waves of emotion, though alluring, are but fleeting reflections on the surface. Beneath this ephemeral facade lies a reservoir of profound understanding—an understanding that love is not confined to moments, but is a force that transcends time, flowing like an eternal river.

As the birds converse and navigate through the challenges of the valley, the readers become fellow travelers, sharing in their experiences and revelations. Through this shared journey, Attar beckons them to rise above the mundane, to embrace a broader, more encompassing form of love that mirrors the universe's own rhythm. It is a call to become attuned to the symphony of the cosmos, where the threads of love weave through every living being and every corner of creation.

This valley's lessons are manifold: that love, when kindled in the heart, is not merely a fleeting sensation, but a radiant flame that lights the path of the seeker. It is a force that dissolves the barriers of time and space, connecting souls across realms. By transcending the temporal, the birds and readers alike uncover a love that is unburdened by limitations—a love that pulses in harmony with the eternal heartbeat of existence. In the embrace of this valley's teachings, the reader is poised to transcend the ordinary, to journey through the transformative fires of love's trials, emerging as a seeker of profound understanding. From the superficial ripples of emotion, they rise to the serene depths of enduring connection, aligning their spirits with the universal cadence that reverberates through the cosmos—an eternal dance of love.

Within this valley, the reader is called to ascend from the shallows of superficial emotions to the depths of profound understanding. The transient yearnings of the heart are met with the call to embrace an enduring, eternal form of love. Through contemplation and connection, the birds and readers alike are urged to transcend the temporal, embracing a love that resonates with the eternal rhythm of the universe.

As the Valley of Love unfurls its secrets, Attar's poem is bathed in the ethereal radiance of spiritual insight. Here, the seeker is not merely an observer but an active participant, invited to peer into the kaleidoscope of love's myriad dimensions. In this realm, love is not just an incidental emotion; it's the very force that propels the journey toward divine union—an unceasing current that drives the seeker forward. Within this valley, where allegorical birds tread a path of extreme significance, an unseen hand extends to readers, beckoning them to venture inward. The layers of the heart are unveiled, much like petals unfurling under the gentle touch of dawn. The currents of love, binding all existence in a harmonious embrace, are revealed as the quintessential essence that transcends both time and form.

In this journey through the Valley of Love, the seeker's perspective shifts. It becomes a pilgrimage of the heart, where emotions are no longer fleeting shadows, but rather, the lanterns guiding the way toward a greater understanding. Love, once seen through the prism of superficiality, now radiates with the brilliance of universality. It's a symphony that harmonizes every note of creation, a thread interwoven into the very fabric of existence. As readers follow the birds' flight, they become companions in this expedition of the soul. The valley's beauty lies not only in its picturesque landscapes but in the profound truths it mirrors. Each step is a revelation—a reminder that love is not confined to the pages of a poem, but a living, breathing force that transcends the boundaries of both the written word and reality itself. The narrative becomes an intricate dance between the allegorical and the personal, the cosmic and the individual. It is an odyssey of recognition, a realization that the very same currents of love that stir the hearts of the allegorical birds also surge within the readers themselves. Love is not a distant concept but a living reality, weaving its magic through every heartbeat, every breath.

As this valley's horizon stretches to meet the seeker's gaze, it invites them to embrace their role as both witness and participant. The ethereal light of spiritual insight bathes the landscape, revealing not just the beauty of the journey, but the profound significance of love as the compass that guides all souls back to their divine source. The birds, allegorical representatives of the seeker's spirit, encounter a pivotal test—the necessity to release their egos and individual identities. This profound trial resonates deeply with the fundamental teachings of Sufism, encapsulated in the concept of "fana," the annihilation of the self to attain unity with the divine. In this juncture of the poem, love ceases to be a mere sentiment; it transforms into a potent instrument for dismantling the walls that stand between souls and the ultimate truth. The journey into the Valley of Love becomes a journey within, where the birds, and by extension, the readers, confront the attachments that bind them to the world of illusions.

The call to release one's ego is a summons to embrace a state of humility, a realization that the self's limitations are but veils that obscure the luminous reality of the divine. As the birds relinquish their individual identities, they become vessels for a higher consciousness, transcending the superficial boundaries that confine them. Love, within this context, becomes a dynamic force—a chisel that chips away at the hardened layers of separation. It's a force that leads the birds to discover that the barriers they once perceived between themselves and others were illusory, dissolving like mist in the light of dawn. The Valley of Love echoes with the resonance of interconnectedness, reminding all that the separation between individuals is merely a transient illusion.

As the birds navigate this profound terrain, they reflect the human struggle to transcend the confines of the ego-driven self. This struggle is not merely a literary device but a reflection of the reader's own journey, their own grappling with the attachments that veil their perception of the divine reality. The Valley of Love's lessons are invitations to recognize the transformative power of love—the power to dissolve the ego and to recognize the interconnectedness that unites all beings.

In this realm, love serves as both a solvent and a bridge—a solvent that dissolves the ego's barriers and a bridge that spans the chasm between the individual soul and the divine essence. The Valley of Love becomes a microcosm of the seeker's greater endeavor, embodying the process of breaking free from the confines of the self and stepping into the boundless expanse of unity.

In traversing this valley's landscapes, the reader journeys through the heart's corridors, exploring the challenges and revelations that the birds encounter. As the birds relinquish their identities, they invite the readers to do the same, opening a gateway to the possibility of unity with the divine—a possibility that blooms from the fertile soil of selfless love.

In the heart of this Valley, an unspoken decree emerges—a demand for sacrifice. Here, the essence of love is not merely a sentiment to be cherished, but a call that resonates with the very core of existence. Just as the birds that journey through this realm must unfurl their wings and release their personal desires and attachments, so too must seekers of the divine detach themselves from the allure of material pursuits and embark on a journey of inner refinement. The call to detach is a whisper that echoes through the very fabric of this valley, a reminder that the path of love is paved with relinquishment. The birds' relinquishing of their desires mirrors the human struggle to relinquish the grip of worldly attachments—attachments that, like anchors, weigh down the soul's ascent.

The trials that the birds encounter in this valley are not mere happenstance; they are profound metaphors for the hardships that accompany the seeker's journey towards spiritual maturity. These hardships mirror the arduous yet transformative challenges that characterize the path of growth—a journey often fraught with uncertainties, yet leading to profound revelations.

The Valley of Love becomes a mirror, reflecting the seeker's own trials and tribulations. Just as the birds' sacrifices guide them towards a higher state of being, the seeker's sacrifices and purifications facilitate a deeper connection with the divine essence. It's a process akin to refining gold—requiring the heat of trials to burn away the impurities of the ego and material desires, leaving behind the purity of the heart's devotion. Sacrifice in this context is not a mere renunciation of the world, but a relinquishment of the self's hold on the temporal, a recognition that the path to unity with the divine demands surrender. The birds' challenges resonate with the reader's own struggles, acting as a mirror that reflects the trials and triumphs of the spiritual journey.

In navigating the hardships of the Valley of Love, the birds mirror the reader's experiences, guiding them to confront their own attachments and embark on the path of inner transformation. Through these allegorical experiences, seekers recognize that purification and sacrifice are not simply requirements, but integral components of the journey—an alchemical process that transmutes the seeker's essence from base to sublime.

Ultimately, the Valley of Love serves as a crucible of growth, where seekers learn that the journey of love is not a leisurely stroll, but a pilgrimage of the soul. As the birds let go and rise above their desires, they embody the essence of sacrifice that paves the way for a closer communion with the divine. In the seeker's own journey, the valley's lessons become a guiding light, a testament to the transformative power of love, purification, and sacrifice.

Amidst the enigmatic landscapes of the Valley of Love, a profound revelation dawns upon the allegorical birds—the realization of the intricate interweaving of all existence. Through their journey, love emerges not only as a personal sentiment but as a celestial thread that unites them with their fellow travelers and, more remarkably, with the boundless expanse of the universe itself.

As the birds progress through this transformative realm, they grasp the profound truth that love is not merely a solitary emotion but a harmonizing force that binds them to others and to the grand tapestry of creation. Love, in its essence, is a radiant bridge connecting souls, transcending the barriers of time and space.

In this valley, the birds' experiences echo the reader's own awakening to the concept of 'oneness," a cornerstone of spiritual understanding found across various traditions. The very fabric of existence is woven with threads of unity—each soul, each being, each element a note in the cosmic symphony. The birds' journey becomes a mirror, reflecting the interconnectedness that lies within the seeker's own heart.

The concept of "oneness," often termed "tawhid," resonates through the Valley of Love's teachings. Just as the birds recognize their shared purpose and destiny, the reader is reminded of the profound interconnectedness that underlies all aspects of life. It's a recognition that beyond the apparent diversity of forms lies a deeper unity, an acknowledgment that all beings originate from the same divine source.

Love, within this context, becomes a profound tool for the seeker—an instrument for recognizing the threads that connect them to their fellow beings, to nature, and to the divine essence. It's a reminder that when love flows freely, barriers crumble, and the heart resonates with the harmonious rhythm of the universe.

In the Valley of Love, the reader's perspective expands, encompassing not only the allegorical birds' journey but their own daily encounters. The interconnectedness that the birds experience becomes a lens through which the reader views their own life, relationships, and interactions. The valley's teachings ripple through their thoughts and actions, inspiring a deeper reverence for the unity that binds all existence.

As the birds traverse the landscape of this valley, they unfurl their wings of understanding, soaring into a realm where love knows no bounds. And just as the birds' experiences mirror the reader's journey, the valley's revelations echo the reader's own discovery—the profound truth that love is the universal force that knits together the vast tapestry of life.

In the heart of the Valley of Love, love takes on a different hue—it transforms into a potent yearning that courses through the allegorical birds' very beings. Their yearning, palpable and fervent, echoes with a resonance that extends beyond their individual desires. It becomes a mirror, reflecting the reader's own yearning for the divine—a yearning that, like an eternal flame, burns within every seeker's heart. The birds' yearning for the Simorgh, the mythical king of birds, stands as a metaphor, mirroring the reader's unquenchable thirst for the divine truth. This theme of longing is not just a literary device; it's a glimpse into the very essence of the spiritual journey. The Valley of Love becomes a testament to the fact that the path of the seeker is not defined solely by the destination, but by the yearning itself—a yearning that kindles hope, fuels perseverance, and lends meaning to every step taken.

The allegorical birds, as they traverse this valley's trials and tribulations, become messengers of a profound truth—that the seeker's yearning is a sacred compass, guiding them through the labyrinthine journey of the soul. Just as the birds' yearning for the Simorgh drives them to face challenges and uncertainties, so too does the seeker's yearning for the divine infuse them with the strength to overcome obstacles. The theme of yearning in the Valley resonates deeply with the reader, for it encapsulates the essence of their own spiritual journey. It's a recognition that the seeker's quest is not defined solely by the destination, but by the yearning itself—a yearning that kindles hope, fuels perseverance, and lends meaning to every step taken.

Amidst the allegorical flights and encounters, the Valley of Love becomes a mirror to the reader's aspirations, inviting them to reflect on the nature of their own yearning. It's a reminder that even in the face of challenges and doubts, the yearning remains as an unwavering beacon, guiding the seeker through the intricate passages of the soul's journey. In this valley, love is not a passive emotion; it's a dynamic force, an unyielding current that stirs the depths of the heart. The birds' yearning mirrors the reader's own longing, and both stand as tributes to the power of inner yearning—a force that transforms the ordinary into the extraordinary and emboldens the seeker to traverse the valleys of life, guided by the luminous light of love's yearning.

As the allegorical birds make their way through the internal of the Valley of Love, a subtle yet profound metamorphosis begins to take shape within them. This transformation, akin to the alchemical process of transmuting ordinary substances into gold, serves as a potent metaphor that echoes the seeker's own passage toward spiritual enlightenment. At the heart of this transformation lies love—a catalyst of unparalleled potency that ushers in this profound change.

The journey through the Valley of Love unveils a journey within—a journey where the birds, representatives of the human spirit, undergo a subtle yet unmistakable shift in their essence. It is as though they shed their mundane feathers, revealing the radiant plumage of their true selves. This transformation mirrors the alchemical concept of transmutation, where base elements are refined to reveal their inherent brilliance.

Just as alchemists endeavor to turn lead into gold, seekers embark on an inner quest to transmute their inner state, to elevate their spiritual essence from the mundane to the divine. This inner alchemy, emblematic of the Valley of Love, is illuminated by the profound power of love. Love serves as the alchemical elixir, catalyzing this metamorphosis and guiding the seeker towards a state of heightened awareness and understanding. The transformation that unfolds within the birds is not a mere narrative embellishment; it resonates deeply with the reader's own journey. The Valley of Love becomes a mirror to the reader's aspirations, reminding them that just as love kindles a transmutative process within the allegorical birds, so too does it ignite the fires of change within the seeker's own heart. Love, within this context, is not merely a sentiment; it's the driving force that urges the seeker to embark on the path of inner alchemy. It's the yearning that propels the journey toward transformation, a yearning that acts as the forge where the base elements of the self are transmuted into the radiant gold of spiritual realization.

As the birds undergo this internal transmutation, readers are invited to contemplate their own inner alchemical journey. The Valley of Love's teachings reverberate, reminding them that the journey of spiritual enlightenment is not a passive endeavor but an active and transformative process—a process fueled by love's luminous flame. In traversing this valley's terrain, both the allegorical birds and the reader become alchemists of the soul. Through love's catalytic power, they discover the profound truth that the seeker's journey is not solely about external exploration, but an internal journey of metamorphosis. Just as the birds' transformation is an embodiment of love's alchemy, so too is the reader's journey a testament to the transformative magic of love's embrace.

In essence, the Valley of Love in "The Conference of the Birds" represents a stage of the spiritual journey that encompasses a rich tapestry of themes and teachings within the Sufi tradition. It encourages readers to explore the depths of love's transformative power, the need for selflessness, and the interconnectedness of all existence. Through its nuanced portrayal of love, this valley invites contemplation on the profound spiritual truths that underlie human experience.

In the Valley of Love, love emerges as a powerful force of transformation. It transcends mere emotion, serving as a catalyst for profound inner change. This love has the remarkable ability to dissolve the ego, that sense of self that often separates individuals from one another and from the divine. Through the transformative power of love, seekers shed their ego-driven identities and awaken to a higher state of consciousness, navigating the intricate path toward spiritual realization.

Detachment and surrender are central themes within the valley. It emphasizes the importance of detaching from worldly attachments and surrendering to a higher spiritual purpose. Detachment doesn't necessitate renouncing the world but rather freeing the heart from the shackles of attachment, allowing for a deeper connection with the eternal.

The valley also illuminates the interconnectedness of all existence. Love acts as a bridge, uniting beings and fostering a profound sense of unity with the universe. Recognizing this interconnectedness cultivates empathy, compassion, and a sense of responsibility toward all of creation.

The birds' intense yearning for the Simorgh symbolizes the seeker's burning, soul-deep longing to reunite with the source of all truth and beauty. This yearning becomes the driving force that propels the seeker through the challenges of the spiritual path, inspiring devotion and giving profound meaning to their quest.

Love's transformative power is akin to the alchemical process of transmutation, where base elements are refined to reveal their divine essence. The seeker undergoes an inner alchemical transformation, characterized by the dissolution of impurities and the emergence of a purified, awakened consciousness.

The valley underscores the importance of sacrifice and purification on the spiritual journey. Sacrifice, in this context, is not about suffering but about willingly letting go of that which impedes spiritual growth. It is through this process of purification that the seeker becomes receptive to the divine presence.

Love serves as a guiding light on the spiritual journey, illuminating the path and providing strength and inspiration to overcome challenges and uncertainties. In moments of doubt or darkness, love acts as a beacon, reminding the seeker of their purpose and the boundless grace of the divine.

The valley encourages the recognition of oneness with all existence, transcending the illusions of separation. Love is the force that binds all beings, reminding the seeker of their essential unity with the universe. This realization leads to a profound sense of compassion, fostering the understanding that to harm another is to harm oneself.

In summary, the Valley of Love in "The Conference of the Birds" is a profound source of spiritual wisdom. It portrays love as a transformative force that guides seekers through the complexities of the inner and outer worlds. These lessons resonate not only with Sufi teachings but with universal spiritual truths, offering profound insights into the nature of human existence and the journey toward enlightenment. Ultimately, this valley invites readers to embark on their own inner pilgrimage, guided by the radiant light of love and a yearning for divine truth.

CHAPTER 12

Transcending the Superficial: A Comprehensive Exploration of the Valley of Knowledge

The Valley of Insight into Mystery or simplified Valley of Knowledge serves as a pivotal and profound stage in the spiritual odyssey of the avian protagonists. This valley, which lies along the path of their quest to find the elusive Simorgh, symbolizes the arduous pursuit of intellectual and spiritual enlightenment. Within its depths, the birds encounter a series of challenges and transformative lessons, each designed to refine their understanding and refine their souls.

As the birds enter the Valley of Knowledge, they are immediately surrounded by an atmosphere of contemplation and introspection. This valley represents a realm where the external distractions of the world fall away, allowing the seekers to turn their focus inward, towards the illumination of wisdom. It is a place where worldly attachments and superficial desires are set aside in favor of the pursuit of higher truths.

The birds' entrance into the Valley marks a profound shift in their spiritual journey, as they step into an environment saturated with an aura of contemplation and introspection. This valley serves as a pivotal stage on their quest for the Simorgh, where the bustling distractions of the external world fade into insignificance. Instead, they are enveloped by an atmosphere that beckons them to turn their gaze inward, toward the radiant light of wisdom and understanding. Here, the valley becomes a sacred sanctuary where the allure of worldly attachments and superficial desires loses its grip on the seekers, paving the way for the pursuit of higher truths and deeper meaning.

As the birds venture further into the Valley of Knowledge, they find themselves in a space that feels almost ethereal—a place where the cacophony of mundane concerns gradually gives way to the gentle whisper of profound questions. The external noise of the world, with its materialistic ambitions and transient pleasures, fades into the background, allowing the birds to divest themselves of the burdens of attachment to worldly possessions and desires.

In this valley, the birds begin to experience a sense of detachment from the fleeting pleasures and ephemeral treasures that once preoccupied their minds. The allure of superficial desires, such as wealth, power, or vanity, loses its luster in the face of a greater purpose—the pursuit of higher truths and spiritual enlightenment. As they progress through the valley, the birds come to understand that true fulfillment lies not in the accumulation of material possessions but in the nourishment of the soul through the acquisition of wisdom and the deepening of their spiritual connection.

The Valley of Knowledge beckons the seekers to engage in introspection and self-examination, a process that encourages them to strip away the layers of external influences and societal expectations. Here, they are invited to confront their innermost thoughts, fears, and aspirations, fostering a profound sense of self-awareness. This introspective journey unveils the deeper recesses of their consciousness, allowing them to see their true selves more clearly and understand the motives and desires that have driven them thus far.

Within the valley's serene ambiance, the birds gradually develop an appreciation for the simple and profound beauty of the pursuit of knowledge and wisdom. They come to realize that the intrinsic value of this pursuit transcends the ephemeral nature of worldly gains and is instead rooted in the eternal and transcendent realm of the intellect and the spirit.

The Valley of Knowledge, thus, stands as a symbolic realm where the birds experience a profound shift in consciousness. It is a place where the worldly distractions and attachments that once held sway over their hearts and minds are gracefully set aside. Here, in this sanctuary of introspection and contemplation, they find the clarity of purpose and the inner strength to continue their spiritual journey, driven by the pursuit of higher truths and the illumination of wisdom. The valley serves as a powerful reminder that the quest for understanding and spiritual growth often necessitates a turning inward, away from the fleeting external world, in order to find the enduring treasures that lie within the depths of the soul.

The Valley is characterized by its remarkable diversity of terrain, each segment serving as a distinctive trial of the birds' unwavering dedication to their quest. It is within these varying landscapes that the birds are confronted with the multifaceted challenges associated with acquiring knowledge, as each part of the valley symbolizes a unique aspect of their intellectual and spiritual growth.

In some sections of the Valley of Knowledge, the terrain becomes rugged and treacherous, reflecting the formidable challenges that are an inherent part of the pursuit of wisdom. Here, the birds must traverse landscapes that are metaphorically strewn with doubts, skepticism, and formidable intellectual obstacles. These treacherous paths represent the difficulties encountered in the quest for profound understanding.

The rugged and uneven ground forces the birds to tread with caution, as they navigate the precipitous slopes of skepticism and uncertainty. They encounter scholars and philosophers who serve as intellectual gatekeepers, challenging the birds' preconceived notions and inviting them to reevaluate their beliefs and perspectives. These encounters become pivotal moments of growth, where the birds are compelled to engage in deep and often challenging dialogues with those who question their assumptions.

The scholars and philosophers they encounter in this part of the valley are not adversaries but rather catalysts for intellectual evolution. They stimulate critical thinking and encourage the birds to venture beyond the confines of their comfort zones. In these exchanges, the birds must summon the courage to confront their own limitations and biases, opening themselves to the transformative power of intellectual exploration.

This segment of the valley teaches the birds that the path to true knowledge is not a straight and unobstructed road but one fraught with obstacles and uncertainties. It underscores the importance of resilience and determination in the face of intellectual challenges. The birds learn that, in the pursuit of knowledge, it is not enough to simply possess information; they must also possess the ability to critically assess and adapt their beliefs based on new insights and perspectives.

Ultimately, the rugged and treacherous terrain of this part of the Valley of Knowledge symbolizes the crucible of intellectual growth. It is a place where the birds grapple with the complexities of knowledge acquisition, confront their doubts and limitations, and emerge with a deeper and more nuanced understanding of the world and themselves. As they progress through this challenging terrain, the birds become not only wiser but also more resilient, better equipped to face the subsequent trials and revelations that await them on their sacred journey towards the Simorgh.

In another enchanting section of the Valley of Knowledge, the landscape undergoes a striking transformation, revealing lush and vibrant gardens that symbolize the joys and pleasures of intellectual exploration. This part of the valley is a veritable paradise for the birds, where they experience the exhilaration of discovering new ideas and insights, basking in the resplendent beauty of knowledge. However, as they revel in the richness of this intellectual oasis, they come to understand that the pursuit of knowledge is not without its own set of trials, as the thirst for wisdom can be both a source of profound joy and a wellspring of profound suffering.

The gardens in this segment of the valley teem with the fruits of intellectual curiosity, their bountiful branches laden with the sweet fruits of discovery and insight. The birds delight in plucking the ripest ideas and savoring the flavors of newfound knowledge. Here, they experience the euphoria of intellectual expansion, the rush of connecting the dots between previously disparate concepts, and the intoxication of learning and growing.

The vibrant gardens also serve as a stark contrast to the rugged terrain encountered earlier in the valley. They represent the rewards of perseverance and the gratification of overcoming intellectual challenges. The birds revel in the sense of accomplishment that accompanies the exploration of new vistas of understanding, and they are reminded that the journey itself, marked by moments of joy and discovery, is a significant part of the pursuit of knowledge.

Yet, even amidst the intoxicating beauty and delight of the gardens, the birds come to realize that the thirst for wisdom can also be a source of suffering. The pursuit of knowledge often brings with it the weight of responsibility—the responsibility to apply that knowledge wisely and ethically, to share it with others, and to grapple with the complexities and moral dilemmas it may unearth. This understanding deepens their appreciation for the profound moral and ethical dimensions of wisdom.

Throughout their journey in this captivating segment of the Valley of Knowledge, the birds have the privilege of encountering a diverse array of guides and mentors. These wise beings, who represent the embodiment of accumulated human knowledge and spiritual insight, become invaluable companions on their journey. These mentors offer guidance, share their own wisdom, and provide valuable lessons that illuminate the path to enlightenment.

In the presence of these mentors, the birds are enriched not only by the wisdom they impart but also by the depth of their compassion and their commitment to the spiritual growth of the seekers. These interactions underscore the interconnectedness of all beings on the quest for wisdom and serve as a testament to the importance of learning from those who have traversed the path before.

This segment of the Valley of Knowledge, thus, represents a captivating interlude in the birds' spiritual journey, where they revel in the delights of intellectual exploration and uncover the beauty of knowledge. It serves as a reminder that the pursuit of wisdom is both a source of joy and a challenge, and that the journey itself is as significant as the destination. The mentors encountered here further enrich their understanding, guiding them toward a deeper connection with the divine and a profound appreciation for the transformative power of knowledge.

Within the captivating expanse of the Valley of Knowledge, where the pursuit of wisdom and enlightenment is paramount, the birds encounter not only the rewards of intellectual exploration but also the ever-present dangers of ego, arrogance, and the temptation to hoard knowledge for personal gain. These pitfalls and distractions serve as crucial lessons, reminding the avian pilgrims that the noble quest for knowledge must be undertaken with a heart guided by humility and a spirit attuned to the greater good of the community.

As the birds progress deeper into the valley, they must remain vigilant against the allure of ego and arrogance. The acquisition of knowledge can be intoxicating, and the temptation to believe oneself superior or infallible in the face of newfound wisdom is a constant threat. The valley teaches them that intellectual pride can blind them to the true essence of knowledge, turning it into a mere tool for self-aggrandizement rather than a path to enlightenment.

Furthermore, the valley serves as a stark reminder that hoarding knowledge for personal gain or power is a disservice to the higher purpose of wisdom. The birds learn that true knowledge should not be sequestered but shared, for it is in sharing that knowledge multiplies and benefits the broader community. This lesson underscores the interconnectedness of all beings and the collective responsibility to foster a society that values and promotes the pursuit of wisdom for the betterment of all.

As the birds progress through the Valley of Knowledge, they undergo a profound transformation of the self. The challenges they face and the lessons they learn act as catalysts for shedding the layers of ignorance and ego that had previously obscured their perception. They come to understand that genuine knowledge is not a mere accumulation of facts and information but a dynamic process of growth and self-discovery.

True knowledge, they realize, is about cultivating wisdom—a deep and profound understanding that transcends the boundaries of the intellect. It encompasses not only the acquisition of knowledge but also the application of that knowledge in ways that foster compassion, empathy, and a deeper connection to the world and its mysteries. The valley guides them toward the recognition that wisdom is a harmonious blend of intellectual insight and spiritual awareness.

In this transformation, the birds come to appreciate the value of humility as an essential companion on the path to enlightenment. They understand that humility allows them to approach knowledge with an open heart and a receptive mind, acknowledging that they are forever students of the universe. They learn that the pursuit of knowledge is not an end in itself but a means to a greater understanding of the world and their place within it.

Ultimately, the Valley of Knowledge serves as a crucible where the birds confront the dual nature of knowledge—it can be a source of both enlightenment and ego, a path to both self-discovery and self-aggrandizement. Through their experiences in this valley, they emerge not only as wiser beings but also as humbler and more compassionate individuals, committed to the noble pursuit of wisdom for the greater good of all beings and the revelation of the divine mysteries that lie ahead.

The Valley of Knowledge, in its essence, symbolizes the transformative power of intellectual and spiritual growth. It teaches us that the journey towards enlightenment is not a straightforward path, but one filled with trials and tribulations. It emphasizes the importance of humility, perseverance, and the willingness to question one's beliefs as essential attributes on the path to true understanding. In this valley, the birds learn that knowledge is not an end in itself but a means to a greater, more profound spiritual awakening, bringing them closer to the ultimate goal of finding the Simorgh and discovering their own inner truth.

SEEKING WISDOM

This pivotal stage in their journey is where they undergo a profound awakening to the indispensable role of knowledge and wisdom in their quest for the Simorgh, realizing that the attainment of their ultimate goal is intrinsically tied to a deeper comprehension of themselves and the vast world that envelops them. As the birds venture further into this valley, they become acutely aware that their initial enthusiasm and zeal for the quest, while admirable, must be complemented by a more profound form of understanding. They recognize that the Simorgh, the symbolic representation of divine truth and unity, cannot be encountered with superficial intentions or ignorance. In this Valley, they begin to comprehend that to reach their goal, they must embark on an inner journey as well as an outer one—a journey of self-discovery and intellectual exploration. Here, the birds encounter a series of enigmatic challenges and revelations that serve as crucibles for their evolving understanding. The valley's diverse landscapes and experiences mirror the multifaceted nature of wisdom itself. They traverse arid deserts of doubt and uncertainty, navigating through the arduous terrain of introspection and self-doubt. In these moments of vulnerability, they confront their own limitations and the depth of their ignorance.

Conversely, the valley also offers fertile oases of insight and enlightenment, where the birds drink deeply from the wellspring of knowledge. They engage in profound conversations with sages and philosophers who impart timeless wisdom, encouraging the seekers to question, reflect, and expand their mental horizons. The birds begin to realize that wisdom is not a stagnant pool but a flowing river that continually nourishes the soul. As they continue their journey through this Valley, the birds uncover the interconnectedness of knowledge and self-awareness.

They understand that wisdom is not merely the accumulation of facts but a holistic integration of knowledge, empathy, and spirituality. It is the bridge that links their individual consciousness to the broader tapestry of existence, facilitating a deeper connection with the world around them.

Furthermore, the valley teaches them the value of humility and the necessity of surrendering their egos in the pursuit of wisdom. They grasp that true wisdom is not a possession to be hoarded but a gift to be shared with others, illuminating the path for fellow seekers. In doing so, they recognize the importance of community and collective growth, for the journey towards wisdom is one that is enriched by the exchange of insights and experiences.

The Valley of Knowledge serves as a transformative crucible for the birds, shaping them into more enlightened beings. It instills in them the understanding that wisdom is not an endpoint but an ever-evolving process—a journey in itself. Armed with this newfound realization, the avian pilgrims continue their quest for the Simorgh, fortified by the conviction that their pursuit of knowledge and wisdom is not just a means to an end, but an integral part of the divine journey toward unity and enlightenment.

REFLECTING ON THEIR OWN EXPERIENCE

In the midst of their journey through the Valley of Knowledge, the birds find themselves in a profound and contemplative state. It is here that they pause to reflect deeply upon the experiences they have accumulated on their arduous quest for the Simorgh. This moment of introspection is a pivotal turning point, as it allows them to connect the dots between their personal experiences and the broader spiritual journey they are undertaking.

As the birds reflect on their own individual paths, they begin to discern patterns and themes that resonate with the broader quest for enlightenment. Each bird's unique journey becomes a microcosm of the larger spiritual odyssey they collectively share. They recognize that their challenges, doubts, and triumphs mirror the challenges and triumphs of all seekers in their pursuit of spiritual understanding.

The Valley of Knowledge serves as a sacred space for this introspection, offering a tranquil and introspective atmosphere where the birds can delve deep into their own consciousness. Here, the birds realize that their encounters with scholars and philosophers, the obstacles they've faced, and the moments of enlightenment they've experienced are not isolated incidents but interconnected threads in the tapestry of their spiritual growth.

In this valley, they come to understand that the pursuit of knowledge and wisdom is not a linear or uniform journey. It is a multifaceted process, and each individual's path is uniquely shaped by their own experiences and insights. Some birds may have faced moments of doubt and skepticism, challenging their beliefs and forcing them to confront their own limitations. Others may have reveled in the joy of intellectual discovery, finding ecstasy in the acquisition of knowledge.

As they share their personal stories and revelations with one another, the birds find a profound sense of camaraderie and unity. They realize that their diverse experiences enrich the collective wisdom of the group, and that in sharing their stories, they strengthen the bonds of community and support. This collective reflection reinforces the idea that the pursuit of knowledge is not a solitary endeavor but a shared pilgrimage towards a common goal.

Furthermore, the birds' reflections in the Valley of Knowledge deepen their appreciation for the interconnectedness of all beings and the importance of empathy and compassion in their journey. They begin to see how their individual growth and self-awareness contribute to the greater tapestry of existence, aligning with the core themes of unity and interconnectedness that underpin their quest for the Simorgh.

The Valley of Knowledge, therefore, serves as a pivotal stage in the birds' spiritual journey, where they pause to reflect on their own experiences and recognize the profound connection between their individual paths and the broader quest for enlightenment. This introspective moment deepens their sense of community, enriches their collective wisdom, and reinforces their commitment to the ultimate goal of finding the Simorgh and attaining spiritual fulfillment. It is a testament to the transformative power of self-reflection and the significance of personal experiences in the pursuit of higher understanding

OVERCOMING INTELLECTUAL CHALLENGES

In the expansive and intellectually stimulating Valley of Knowledge, the birds face a myriad of intellectual challenges and philosophical dilemmas that test the very essence of their being. As they progress along their spiritual journey, they grapple with profound questions that probe the nature of reality, existence, and the Divine. Here, the pursuit of knowledge is not merely an academic exercise but a profound inquiry into the fundamental mysteries of existence.

The valley presents the birds with a formidable array of philosophical quandaries. They find themselves immersed in debates about the nature of reality itself. Are the experiences they encounter on their journey mere illusions or glimpses of a deeper truth? Is the world they perceive an accurate reflection of reality, or is there more to existence than meets the eye? These questions challenge the birds to question the very foundations of their understanding and confront the limitations of human perception.

In their pursuit of answers, the birds engage in contemplation and deep introspection. They withdraw from the distractions of the external world and turn inward, exploring the depths of their own consciousness. This inner journey allows them to peel away the layers of conventional knowledge and societal conditioning, seeking a more profound connection with the mysteries of existence.

Conversations with fellow seekers and the wise beings they encounter in the valley become a crucial part of their quest for understanding. Through dialogue and discourse, they exchange ideas and perspectives, often encountering viewpoints that challenge their preconceived notions. These dialogues are not mere intellectual exercises but profound opportunities for growth and transformation, as the birds learn to embrace the diversity of thought and perspective that enriches their collective wisdom.

The valley also introduces the birds to the concept of the Divine and its enigmatic nature. They grapple with questions about the existence and nature of God, asking whether the Divine is a separate entity or an inherent aspect of their own being. These inquiries lead them to explore the depths of spirituality and the interconnectedness of all things, bridging the gap between philosophy and mysticism.

Amidst the intellectual challenges, the birds experience moments of profound insight and revelation. They come to understand that the pursuit of knowledge is not solely an exercise in intellectual conquest but a means to attain a deeper, more intimate connection with the Divine. They realize that the answers to their philosophical inquiries are not always straightforward and that the journey itself, marked by exploration and contemplation, is as significant as the destination.

Ultimately, the Valley of Knowledge becomes a crucible of intellectual growth and spiritual evolution for the birds. It teaches them the value of embracing uncertainty and ambiguity as they grapple with the profound mysteries of existence. It reminds them that the pursuit of knowledge is a lifelong endeavor, one that requires humility, curiosity, and a willingness to engage with the profound questions that define the human experience.

As they emerge from this valley, the birds are not only intellectually enriched but spiritually transformed. They carry with them a deeper understanding of reality, a more profound connection to the Divine, and an unwavering commitment to their quest for the Simorgh. The Valley of Knowledge becomes a testament to the birds' resilience in the face of intellectual challenges and their unwavering determination to seek the truth, no matter how elusive it may be.

DEVELOPING SPIRITUAL INSIGHTS

In the profound and transformative journey through the Valley of Knowledge, the birds undergo a profound evolution in their understanding of spiritual insight and discernment. This valley becomes a crucible in which they learn to distinguish between superficial knowledge and true wisdom, realizing that spiritual knowledge transcends mere facts and theories. Here, they embark on a spiritual quest that transcends the boundaries of conventional understanding.

As the birds progress through the Valley of Knowledge, they come to understand that the pursuit of spiritual insight is not limited to the accumulation of facts or the recitation of dogma. Instead, they recognize that it entails a deep and personal engagement with the mysteries of existence. This understanding prompts them to move beyond the mere acquisition of information and toward a more profound exploration of the self and the cosmos.

One of the key lessons they glean from this valley is that spiritual insight requires introspection and contemplation. They learn that true wisdom is not found in the external world but arises from within, as they delve into the depths of their own consciousness. By engaging in self-reflection, meditation, and mindfulness, the birds begin to uncover the inner truths that lie beyond the surface of everyday experience.

In their interactions with wise beings and fellow seekers, the birds also discover the value of dialogue and shared experience. They come to understand that spiritual insight is enriched through the exchange of ideas and perspectives. These dialogues serve as a crucible for testing their own understanding and challenging their preconceptions. They learn to approach discussions with an open heart and a receptive mind, recognizing that the truest insights often arise through the fusion of diverse viewpoints.

Moreover, the Valley of Knowledge impresses upon the birds the importance of humility in their quest for spiritual insight. They realize that arrogance and ego can obstruct the path to wisdom. By humbling themselves and acknowledging the vastness of what they do not know, they become more receptive to the profound teachings of the valley and the wisdom that lies beyond.

Through their journey, the birds also discover that spiritual insight is not static but ever-evolving. It is not a destination but a continuous process of growth and refinement. They recognize that the pursuit of wisdom is a lifelong endeavor, one that requires patience, perseverance, and an unwavering commitment to inner transformation.

In this valley, the birds come to appreciate the interconnectedness of all knowledge and wisdom. They understand that spiritual insight transcends the boundaries of individual disciplines or belief systems. It is a universal truth that can be found in the teachings of various traditions and the experiences of diverse cultures. They learn to see the common threads that unite all seekers in their quest for higher understanding.

Ultimately, as the birds emerge from the Valley of Knowledge, they carry with them not only a deeper appreciation for the mysteries of existence but also a profound sense of spiritual insight and discernment. They understand that true wisdom is not a possession but a state of being—an ever-deepening connection to the Divine and a heightened awareness of the interconnectedness of all things. This insight becomes a guiding light on their continued journey toward the Simorgh, reminding them that the pursuit of spiritual knowledge is a sacred and transformative pilgrimage of the soul.

LESSONS LEARNED

The Valley of Knowledge, imparts profound and timeless lessons that resonate not only within the context of the allegorical narrative but also in the broader scope of individuals' spiritual journeys. These key lessons, drawn from the experiences of the birds, underscore the significance of continual learning, self-reflection, humility, and the integration of knowledge into one's life. They serve as invaluable guidance for those seeking personal growth and a deeper connection to the divine or their inner selves.

The Valley of Knowledge emphasizes that the pursuit of wisdom is an ongoing journey, devoid of finality. It teaches that learning is not confined to a specific timeframe or age but is a lifelong endeavor. Just as the birds encounter various challenges and lessons along their path, individuals on their spiritual journey must remain open to new insights and experiences, continuously expanding their understanding of the world and themselves.

This Valley underscores the importance of introspection and self-examination. It encourages individuals to turn their gaze inward, exploring the depths of their own consciousness. Through self-reflection, seekers can uncover inner truths, confront their limitations, and gain a clearer understanding of their motivations, fears, and desires. This self-awareness is a fundamental step toward personal growth and spiritual enlightenment.

Humility is a recurring theme in the Valley of Knowledge. The birds learn that arrogance and ego can obstruct the path to wisdom. By acknowledging their own limitations and embracing a sense of humility, individuals become more receptive to the teachings of life and the wisdom that surrounds them. Humility allows seekers to approach their journey with an open heart and a willingness to learn from others, regardless of their background or beliefs.

The valley emphasizes that knowledge is not a mere collection of facts and information but a living, transformative force. To truly benefit from wisdom, individuals must integrate it into their lives. This means embodying the principles and insights they acquire, allowing knowledge to shape their actions, attitudes, and relationships. Integration bridges the gap between theory and practice, ensuring that wisdom becomes a guiding light in daily life.

These key lessons from the Valley of Knowledge resonate with seekers of spiritual enlightenment, as they offer practical guidance for personal growth and a deeper connection to the divine or inner self. By embracing the concept of continual learning, individuals remain open to the mysteries of existence. Through self-reflection, they gain clarity and self-awareness, paving the way for inner transformation. Cultivating humility fosters a sense of openness and receptivity, while the integration of knowledge into one's life ensures that wisdom becomes a guiding force, shaping one's journey towards a deeper understanding of the self and the world. Ultimately, these lessons serve as a testament to the enduring power of wisdom and the transformative potential of the spiritual path.

CHAPTER 13

Valley of Detachment: A Symbol of Cultivating the Inner Richness

The Valley of Detachment in Fariduddin Attar's "The Conference of the Birds" is a profound stage of the birds' spiritual journey, where they learn to relinquish their attachments to the material world and embrace the path of inner transformation. In this valley, the birds confront their desires, illusions, and ego-driven cravings, seeking to attain a state of inner freedom and detachment from worldly distractions.

As the birds venture deeper into the Valley of Detachment, they are greeted by an atmosphere of serene tranquility. The air seems lighter, carrying with it a sense of liberation from the burdens of material possessions and desires. The landscape around them transforms into a blend of vibrant colors and soothing shades, symbolizing the diversity of human experiences that must be integrated to achieve detachment.

The Hoopoe, their wise guide, leads the birds through this valley with a gentle yet firm demeanor, recognizing the challenges they are about to face. The journey unfolds as a series of encounters and experiences that prompt each bird to confront their attachments head-on.

The first challenge that the birds encounter in their journey through the Valley is a lush garden adorned with jewels that sparkle like stars against the night sky. This breathtaking sight awakens a myriad of emotions within the flock—desire, fascination, and even envy. The garden's jewels represent the allure of material wealth and external beauty, which often captivate and distract individuals from their spiritual pursuits.

In this pivotal moment, the Hoopoe, the wise and enlightened leader of the birds, perceives the inner turmoil and conflict arising among the birds due to their attraction to the garden's treasures. The Hoopoe's role in this allegorical tale is crucial as it acts as a spiritual guide and a source of wisdom for the birds throughout their journey. The Hoopoe's words resonate through the garden like a soothing melody, cutting through the birds' desires and distractions. Its speech serves as a gentle yet powerful reminder to the birds, encouraging them to reflect on the ephemeral nature of material possessions and external beauty. The Hoopoe's message carries profound spiritual insights, urging the birds to look beyond the surface and contemplate the deeper meaning of their existence.

The wisdom of the Hoopoe acts as a balm for the pangs of desire that have stirred within the birds. It serves to calm their restless hearts and redirect their focus toward a higher purpose. By guiding the birds to contemplate the transient nature of worldly wealth and beauty, the Hoopoe underscores the Sufi concept of detachment from the material world. This detachment is a fundamental step on the path to spiritual enlightenment and union with the divine. In a broader sense, this encounter with the garden of jewels and the Hoopoe's teachings are relevant to readers today. In a world often dominated by consumerism, the pursuit of material wealth, and the constant bombardment of external beauty ideals, individuals can easily become ensnared in desires and distractions. The Valley of Detachment, represented by this garden scene, serves as a timeless reminder to reflect on our own attachments, desires, and priorities.

The Hoopoe's wisdom encourages readers to question the value of transient possessions and appearances, inviting them to explore the deeper dimensions of their lives. By doing so, readers can find resonance in the message of the Valley and consider their own spiritual journey, seeking inner transformation and a connection to something greater than the fleeting treasures of the external world.

Further along their path, the avian travelers stumble upon a serene pond, its tranquil surface mirroring the clear blue sky above. As the birds gaze into the still waters, they catch sight of their own reflections, and a sense of enchantment washes over them. The allure of their own beauty captivates their hearts, and they become enamored by the images that stare back at them. In this moment, the birds are once again ensnared, but this time by the trap of vanity and ego. The reflections in the pond serve as a stark reminder of how easily individuals can become preoccupied with their external appearances, overly concerned with physical beauty, and fixated on their own egos. Vanity, like a mirage, can divert one from the true path and hinder spiritual progress.

Once more, it is the Hoopoe, the embodiment of wisdom and spiritual guidance, whose voice resounds through the air like a soothing breeze. The Hoopoe's words act as a wake-up call, gently shaking the birds from their reverie of self-absorption. Its message is clear and profound, emphasizing the perilous nature of vanity and ego on the spiritual journey. The Hoopoe urges the birds to look beyond the superficial realm of appearances, imploring them to explore the depths of their souls. It encourages them to seek the essence that transcends the fleeting beauty of their physical forms. In this call to inner reflection, the Hoopoe highlights a core Sufi principle—the importance of self-knowledge and self-realization. True enlightenment is not found in the external world or in the admiration of one's own image; it is discovered through introspection, humility, and the recognition of one's connection to the divine.

The message resonating from the Hoopoe's teachings at the pond is as relevant today as it was in Attar's time. In the contemporary world, where social media and societal pressures often foster a culture of self-absorption and image-consciousness, individuals can easily fall into the trap of ego and vanity. The encounter with the pond serves as a poignant reminder for readers to reflect on their own tendencies towards self-centeredness and to strive for a deeper understanding of their true selves.

The lesson of the pond in the Valley encourages readers to go beyond the surface, to look within their hearts, and to seek the inner truth that transcends the fleeting allure of external appearances. It reminds us all that the path to spiritual enlightenment requires the shedding of ego and vanity, allowing the authentic self to emerge and connect with the divine.

The culmination of the birds' journey through the Valley of Detachment takes them to a serene and contemplative grove, a place of profound stillness and inner peace. Here, the birds find themselves invited to sit and meditate, marking a pivotal moment in their spiritual quest. The grove, with its tranquil atmosphere, represents the ideal setting for self-reflection and introspection—a sanctuary away from the distractions of the external world.

As the birds gather in this sacred space, the Hoopoe continues to serve as their wise and compassionate guide. The Hoopoe's presence is a symbol of spiritual leadership and enlightenment, offering the birds the guidance they need to navigate the challenging terrain of detachment. In this hallowed grove, the Hoopoe encourages the birds to embark on a journey within themselves. They are urged to delve deep into their own hearts and minds, examining the attachments and illusions that have held them captive for so long. This introspective process is not easy; it requires the birds to confront their deepest fears, desires, and insecurities.

One by one, the birds begin to open their hearts and share their inner struggles with the group. They reveal the yearnings that have driven them, the attachments that have bound them, and their deep-seated desire for liberation. Through this process of sharing, the birds find solace in the realization that they are not alone in their journey. They discover a sense of community and unity with their fellow travelers, as they all grapple with similar challenges on their path to spiritual enlightenment.

This communal sharing of vulnerabilities and aspirations serves as a powerful metaphor for the importance of dialogue and mutual support on the spiritual journey. It highlights the significance of seeking guidance and sharing one's innermost thoughts and struggles with trusted mentors or peers. In this context, the Hoopoe embodies the role of a spiritual leader who facilitates this process of self-discovery and transformation.

The scene in the grove also underscores the notion that true detachment is not a cold or heartless separation from the world but a process of inner exploration and understanding. It is about letting go of the attachments that bind the soul while cultivating a deeper connection to one's true self and to the divine.

For readers today, the message from this part of the Birds' journey remains relevant. It encourages individuals to carve out moments of silence and self-reflection in their busy lives, to confront their own attachments and illusions, and to seek guidance and support on their own spiritual journeys. It reminds us all that the path to inner liberation is a shared endeavor, where the sharing of our inner struggles can lead to greater understanding, compassion, and ultimately, transcendence.

As the birds share their stories in the silent grove, a profound and transformative sense of solidarity begins to emerge among them. They realize that the attachments that have bound them are not unique or isolated struggles but universal human experiences. Each bird's tale resonates with the others, creating a deep sense of connection and understanding. This communal sharing reinforces the idea that the journey of detachment is a shared human endeavor, and they are not alone in their quest for spiritual enlightenment.

The Hoopoe, always a source of compassion and wisdom, contributes to this sense of unity by sharing stories of sages and mystics who have also traversed the Valley of Detachment. These narratives illustrate the profound and life-changing impact of detachment on these spiritual seekers. The stories serve as inspirational examples of the transformative power of letting go of worldly attachments and ego, highlighting the possibility of inner liberation and union with the divine.

In this valley, the birds undergo a profound shift in their understanding of detachment. They come to realize that true detachment is not a rejection of the world or an ascetic renunciation of material possessions. Instead, it is about liberating the heart from the suffocating grip of attachments. They grasp the concept that authentic freedom is found in the ability to engage with the material world while remaining untouched by its impermanence. Detachment is not a withdrawal from life but a deeper engagement with it, marked by a sense of inner tranquility and equanimity.

As the birds emerge from the Valley of Detachment, they carry with them a renewed sense of purpose and a profound understanding. Their steps are lighter, and their hearts are freer as they continue their journey toward self-realization and union with the Divine. This valley remains a pivotal turning point in their quest, serving as a constant reminder that the path to enlightenment requires letting go of what is fleeting and embracing what is eternal—the inner connection to the divine source that transcends all worldly attachments.

In summary, the Valley of Detachment is a symbolic representation of the human struggle with attachment and the journey towards spiritual liberation. Through the garden, pond, and grove, Attar presents a multi-layered exploration of desires, ego, and the transformative power of self-awareness. The Hoopoe's guidance and the birds' shared experiences illuminate the complexities of the detachment process, ultimately guiding them toward a deeper understanding of inner richness and liberation.

CHAPTER 14

Valley of Unity: A symbol of Spiritual Realization

The Valley of Unity, a pivotal stage in Fariduddin Attar's "Conference of the Birds," serves as a transformative and illuminating phase in the spiritual journey of the avian protagonists. As the birds progress along their arduous path towards the enigmatic Simorgh, this particular valley stands out as a symbol of profound enlightenment and inner realization. The Valley of Unity is where they begin to grasp a central tenet of Sufi philosophy: the concept of unity.

Here in this valley, the birds encounter a shift in their consciousness. They move beyond their limited sense of self and recognize the interconnectedness that binds them not only to each other but to all of existence. The Valley of Unity becomes a place of profound insight, where the birds shed the burdens of their individual egos and worldly attachments. Within this valley, the birds learn that their perceived separation from the Divine is, in reality, an illusion. They come to understand that their individual identities are mere facets of a greater, unified whole. This realization marks a significant turning point in their journey, as they begin to feel a sense of oneness with the Divine and all living beings.

As they traverse the Valley of Unity, the birds begin to see that their true essence is not separate from the Divine but is, in fact, a reflection of it. They experience a heightened awareness of the interconnectedness and interdependence of all existence, a core concept in Sufi mysticism. The valley serves as a crucible for the dissolution of the ego and the emergence of a more profound understanding of their place in the universe.

This transformation is not just intellectual; it is a deep spiritual awakening. The birds' hearts and souls resonate with the profound truth that unity and oneness are the ultimate realities underlying the multifaceted world they have known. This newfound understanding propels them forward on their spiritual journey, bringing them closer to their ultimate destination: union with the Simorgh.

The Valley of Unity, thus, signifies the critical stage in the birds' spiritual journey where they realize the interconnectedness and oneness of all existence. It is a place of profound awakening, where the boundaries of individuality and separation begin to dissolve, allowing the birds to draw closer to their ultimate goal of spiritual union with the Divine. This valley serves as a timeless allegory for the transformative power of recognizing the unity and interconnectedness that underlies the diversity of creation.

As the birds continue their journey through the Valley of Unity, they are greeted by an atmosphere laden with a palpable sense of interconnectedness and oneness. The very air they breathe seems to pulse with a unity that transcends their individual identities. It's in this ethereal setting that they encounter a revelation that shakes the foundation of their perception—the revelation that all they have ever known as separate entities are, in truth, manifestations of the same divine reality.

The Hoopoe, their sage and spiritual guide, steps forward to elucidate the profound truth that permeates this valley. With wisdom flowing from every feather, the Hoopoe explains that the perceived boundaries and divisions that have defined their existence are mere illusions. In the grand tapestry of creation, everything they have considered separate—each tree, each bird, each gust of wind—is, in fact, an expression of the same divine essence.

As the birds listen to the Hoopoe's words, their hearts and minds are touched by a profound revelation. They begin to understand that the diversity they once perceived as division is, in reality, a testament to the infinite facets of the divine reality. Every being and element in the cosmos is a unique note in the grand symphony of existence, each contributing to the harmonious whole.

The Valley of Unity becomes a place of deep introspection and inner transformation. Here, the birds shed the burdens of their individual self and the trappings of worldly attachments. They embrace the truth that unity is not merely an abstract concept but a living, breathing reality that flows through every fiber of the universe.

With this newfound awareness, the birds start to experience a sense of profound connection. They recognize that the same divine essence that resides within them is present in every living creature, in every rock and river. This realization fills their hearts with a deep sense of love, compassion, and empathy for all of creation.

As the birds continue their journey through the Valley of Unity, they do so with a great sense of purpose and unity. The illusory barriers of separation have crumbled, and they are now driven by a shared understanding—a shared truth. They have taken their first steps toward spiritual enlightenment, knowing that the ultimate destination, the Simorgh, is not separate from them but a reflection of the divine reality they now carry within their hearts.

In the Valley of Unity, the birds have discovered a deep truth that will guide them through the remaining stages of their spiritual quest. It is a truth that transcends words and concepts, a truth that can only be fully grasped through direct experience—a truth that unites them with the very essence of existence itself.

In the mystical expanse of the Valley of Unity, the birds on their spiritual odyssey experience an intense state of transcendence that reshapes their understanding of reality. As they venture deeper into this valley, they undergo a transformation that goes beyond mere intellectual comprehension; it is a visceral and spiritual awakening. The boundaries that once rigidly defined their existence—the barriers of ego, the illusions of separateness—begin to dissolve like mist under the warming rays of the sun. These boundaries had previously confined them to narrow perceptions of self and other, bird and mountain, sky and earth. But within the Valley of Unity, these distinctions lose their sharp edges, and the lines that separated them blur, fading into the background of a greater cosmic carpet.

In this state of transcendence, the birds come to a profound realization: they are not isolated individuals but integral components of a vast and interconnected web of existence. The feathers of one bird are intertwined with the leaves of the trees; the songs of the birds harmonize with the rustling of the winds through the valleys; the rhythms of their heartbeats resonate with the heartbeat of the Earth itself.

The concept of "otherness" dissipates as the birds perceive the interwoven threads that connect them to their fellow travelers. What once appeared as distinct entities now becomes threads in the same fabric. The boundaries between the birds' identities begin to blur, and they experience a sense of shared consciousness. They see themselves not as separate beings but as expressions of the same divine reality that flows through all things.

The mountains that once appeared as towering, unyielding obstacles are now recognized as fellow travelers on this cosmic journey. The sky above and the earth below are not separate realms but interconnected aspects of the same boundless universe. The birds recognize that every element of the world around them is not just interconnected but interdependent, each contributing to the harmony of the whole.

As they continue their journey through the Valley of Unity, the birds move with a newfound sense of grace and purpose. They are no longer driven by individual desires and ambitions but by a shared understanding of their place in the grand design of existence. Compassion and empathy blossom within them, for they see themselves in every living being and recognize the same divine spark that ignites their own souls in all of creation.

In this valley of transcendence, the birds touch the very heart of mysticism, where the superficial distinctions of the material world fade into insignificance. They glimpse the profound truth that unity is not an abstract concept but a living reality that can be felt in every breath, every heartbeat, and every moment of existence.

The Valley of Unity becomes a sacred space where the birds have their first taste of the divine union they seek—a union not only with the Simorgh but with the entirety of creation. It is a transformational stage where they shed the illusions of separation, and in doing so, they come one step closer to realizing the ultimate truth of their spiritual quest.

The Valley, for the wise Birds, is an eloquent and evocative representation of a profound spiritual concept—the interconnectedness and oneness of all existence. It serves as a poignant reminder, not only to the birds on their mystical journey but also to readers, to transcend the confines of dualistic thinking and perceive the deeper spiritual truths that underlie the material world.

As the birds venture deeper into the valley, they begin to shed the shackles of dualistic thinking—the tendency to categorize the world into opposites, such as self and other, good and bad, individual and collective. These dichotomies, which often limit human understanding, fall away in the face of a greater realization. The boundaries that once seemed impenetrable start to blur, revealing the interconnected threads that weave together the tapestry of existence. In this state of awakening, the birds perceive that they are not isolated individuals on a solitary quest, but rather integral parts of a grand cosmic symphony. They come to understand that every bird, every creature, every aspect of the natural world, and even the mountains and the skies, are not separate entities but expressions of the same divine essence. The distinctions between self and other dissolve, and a profound sense of unity prevails.

The Valley of Unity challenges the birds to transcend the limitations of their egos and embrace a higher perspective—a perspective that recognizes the inherent oneness of all life. It is a powerful invitation to move beyond the divisive notions of "us" and "them" and to embrace a vision of the world as a unified whole.

For readers of Attar's allegorical masterpiece, the Valley of Unity serves as an inspirational and instructive symbol. It encourages us to reflect on our own lives and perceptions, prompting us to examine the dualities and divisions that we encounter on a daily basis. It reminds us that beneath the surface of apparent multiplicity, there exists a profound unity that connects all living beings.

Ultimately, the Valley of Unity invites us to embark on our own inner journey, to transcend the limitations of dualistic thinking, and to recognize the interconnectedness and oneness of existence. It serves as a timeless reminder that the quest for spiritual enlightenment often involves a shift in consciousness, a shift from perceiving the world through the lens of separation to perceiving it through the lens of unity—a perspective that aligns with the deepest spiritual truths of many wisdom traditions.

SYMBOLISM IN THE VALLEY OF UNITY

The symbolism embedded in the Valley of Unity is indeed a tapestry woven with rich and layered threads of meaning. This allegorical stage in the birds' journey mirrors and embodies the profound Sufi concept of tawhid, which encapsulates the oneness of God and all of creation. It's a concept that has deep roots in Islamic mysticism and holds universal spiritual significance.

In the Valley of Unity, the birds experience a profound transformation that parallels the Sufi understanding of the individual soul's journey toward realizing its intrinsic connection with the divine reality. Just as the birds shed the illusion of separateness, Sufism teaches that the human soul's true nature is fundamentally intertwined with the divine essence. This valley serves as a powerful metaphor for the ultimate spiritual goal in Sufism—the realization of the divine presence within all beings and the recognition of the underlying unity of existence.

The valley's symbolism underscores the core teachings of Sufism:

Tawhid (Oneness):

The Valley of Unity encapsulates the essence of tawhid, which is the cornerstone of Islamic & Sufi philosophy. Just as the birds come to recognize the interconnectedness of all things, Sufism emphasizes the unity of God and creation. It teaches that there is only one ultimate reality, and everything in the universe is a manifestation of that divine reality. This realization is an intense awakening, as the boundaries of duality and separation fall away.

Transcending the Ego:

In the Valley of Unity, the birds undergo a spiritual transformation where they shed their egos and let go of their individual identities. This mirrors the Sufi journey of self-purification and self-negation, where the ego (nafs) is transcended to uncover the deeper, true self (nafs al-amara). The birds' experience serves as a powerful allegory for the process of self-realization and surrender to the divine will.

Interconnectedness:

As the birds recognize their interconnectedness, it echoes the Sufi belief that every soul is connected to the divine source. Sufis often use the metaphor of a drop of water merging back into the ocean to describe this unity. In the Valley of Unity, the birds experience a similar merging, where individuality fades in the face of a greater cosmic oneness.

Divine Essence Within:

The valley serves as a metaphor for the realization that the divine essence resides within all beings. Just as the birds perceive the same divine reality in every aspect of their surroundings, Sufism teaches that the divine is immanent in all of creation. This recognition leads to a deep sense of reverence for all life and a profound love for the Creator.

CONCLUSION

In summary, the Valley of Unity is a profound allegorical representation of key Sufi teachings. It encapsulates the journey from duality to oneness, from ego to divine realization, and from separation to interconnectedness. Through this symbolism, readers are invited to contemplate and internalize the timeless wisdom of Sufi mysticism, which emphasizes the profound truth that the divine reality is both transcendent and immanent, and that the ultimate spiritual goal is the realization of the divine essence within all beings.

The Valley of Unity stands as a pivotal juncture in the epic voyage undertaken by the birds in their relentless pursuit of self-discovery and spiritual enlightenment. Within the verses of the poem, these avian wayfarers embark on a treacherous and profound odyssey, driven by their unwavering quest to locate and unite with their legendary sovereign, the Simorgh, who embodies the quintessential embodiment of truth and spiritual illumination. In this timeless narrative, the Valley of Unity emerges as a profound and symbolic testament to the transformative power of their journey.

As the birds press on, their journey unfolds as a metaphorical pilgrimage, filled with trials and tribulations, each valley they encounter serving as a poignant emblem of distinct stages in their spiritual expedition. Yet, it is the Valley of Unity that emerges as a beacon of profound significance within the tapestry of their quest. Within the depths of this valley, the birds confront a profound revelation—one that beckons them to recognize the intrinsic interconnectedness of all existence. Here, they are challenged to see beyond the illusion of separateness and discern the underlying unity that binds all beings and the universe itself. It is in this valley that they begin to grasp that their individual selves are but drops in the vast ocean of existence, and that true enlightenment lies in embracing this unity.

The Valley of Unity, therefore, stands as a profound metaphor for the transformative power of unity in the birds' spiritual evolution. It represents a pivotal point in their journey where they transcend the limitations of ego and self-interest, recognizing that their quest for the Simorgh and ultimate enlightenment is inseparable from the collective destiny of all beings.

In traversing this valley, the birds undergo a profound metamorphosis of consciousness, shedding the layers of ego and separateness that have bound them in ignorance. Here, they realize that unity is not merely a destination but a fundamental truth that underlies the entire cosmos. It is a realization that propels them further on their path toward self-discovery and spiritual enlightenment. In essence, the Valley of Unity serves as a potent reminder that the pursuit of spiritual enlightenment is not a solitary endeavor but a collective awakening, where the individual's journey toward truth is intimately intertwined with the welfare of all. It encapsulates the profound insight that the ultimate destination of their quest is not a distant realm but a timeless truth that resides within and around them—a truth that they can only grasp through unity, compassion, and the dissolution of the self into the boundless sea of existence. Thus, the Valley of Unity remains a timeless symbol of the transformative power of unity on the birds' journey toward self-realization and spiritual enlightenment.

CHAPTER 15

Valley of Bewilderment: Transition from the comfort of the known to the excitement of discovery

The Valley of Bewilderment is one of the significant stages in Fariduddin Attar's "The Conference of the Birds." This valley represents a pivotal point in the birds' spiritual journey, where they confront the profound state of confusion and perplexity that often accompanies a seeker's path to enlightenment.

As the birds continue their arduous quest to find the Simorgh, they arrive at the Valley of Bewilderment. Here, they are met with an overwhelming sense of confusion and disarray. The landscape itself seems to mirror their inner turmoil, with twisted paths, distorted reflections, and a maze-like terrain that confounds their senses.

In this valley, the birds experience a deep and unsettling Astonishment. Their minds are clouded with uncertainty, doubts, and questions. The Hoopoe, their guide, explains that this valley is a necessary phase of the spiritual journey. It is a test of their perseverance, resilience, and commitment to the path. The Valley of Bewilderment is a symbolic representation of the challenges that seekers often face when delving into the depths of spiritual exploration. It reflects the confusion that arises when one confronts the limitations of the rational mind and grapples with the mysteries of the divine. Just as the physical landscape is disorienting, the mental and emotional landscape of the birds is similarly tumultuous.

The Valley, Attar defines, is a profound metaphor that encapsulates the intricate and often perplexing aspects of the spiritual journey. This mystical valley serves as a poignant symbol for the broader human experience, reflecting the multifaceted nature of our existence and our relentless pursuit of the divine. Much like the birds navigating through this enigmatic terrain, individuals embarking on their spiritual quests frequently encounter moments of bewilderment and profound amazement.

At the heart of this analogy lies the idea that the spiritual journey is not a linear path with clear signposts but a meandering expedition filled with unexpected twists and turns. The Valley of Bewilderment mirrors the ups and downs of life itself, where individuals grapple with questions about the meaning of their existence, the nature of divinity, and the mysteries that lie beyond their understanding. It represents those times when we find ourselves immersed in the wonder of the universe, awestruck by its beauty and complexity, yet simultaneously bewildered by the elusive answers to our deepest inquiries.

In this context, the valley becomes an indispensable part of the spiritual voyage, for it is during these moments of bewilderment that individuals are often pushed to confront their own limitations and seek deeper insights. It is through this dialectic between perplexity and revelation that they can gain a more profound understanding of themselves and their connection to the divine.

Just as the birds in their quest for the valley's elusive secrets must navigate through its twists and turns, individuals on their spiritual journeys must learn to navigate the complexities and paradoxes of their own lives. The Valley teaches us that these moments of uncertainty and astonishment are not detours but integral parts of the path itself. They challenge us to transcend our comfort zones, embrace the unknown, and venture into the depths of our own souls to uncover the profound truths that lie therein.

The Valley, thus, stands as a potent symbol of the human condition and the intricate nature of the spiritual journey. It reminds us that, like the birds in their pursuit of the valley's mysteries, we too must grapple with bewilderment and amazement as we seek to understand our existence and our connection to the divine. Through these experiences, we can ultimately find the wisdom and enlightenment we seek, making the journey itself as valuable as the destination.

In this valley, the birds learn several important lessons in the indispensable role of uncertainty and discomfort in the spiritual odyssey. It stands as a testament to the idea that the pursuit of higher truths demands a willingness to venture beyond the reassuring boundaries of the known and the familiar. In this mystical valley, individuals encounter the crucible of transformation, where the essence of the spiritual journey is distilled into its purest form.

At its core, the Valley of Bewilderment is a symbolic representation of the uncharted territory that seekers of spiritual enlightenment must tread. It is a terrain fraught with ambiguity, where the certainties of conventional understanding are left behind. This valley reminds us that to explore the depths of our spirituality, we must be prepared to relinquish the comfort of the familiar and confront the inherent enigmas of existence.

In the context of the spiritual journey, the valley underscores the notion that genuine growth and enlightenment occur when we step out of our comfort zones. The discomfort experienced within its bewildering confines becomes a catalyst for inner transformation. It is in the midst of uncertainty and disorientation that individuals are compelled to question, reflect, and seek deeper meaning. These moments of bewilderment become the crucible where self-discovery and spiritual evolution take place. Moreover, the Valley of Bewilderment teaches us that the pursuit of higher truths often involves a degree of paradox and contradiction. It is a place where opposites coexist, where darkness and light, doubt and faith, converge. Embracing these paradoxes is a critical aspect of the spiritual journey, as it encourages individuals to transcend dualistic thinking and embrace a more holistic perspective of reality.

In its essence the valley symbolizes the threshold between the known and the unknown, between the comfortable and the challenging. It serves as a reminder that the spiritual path is not a linear ascent but a multidimensional exploration, where growth is achieved through the confrontation of discomfort and the willingness to traverse the bewildering landscapes of the soul. Ultimately, the Valley reminds us that the pursuit of higher truths is a transformative journey that requires courage, resilience, and an openness to the mysteries of existence. It teaches us that by embracing uncertainty and discomfort, we can uncover profound insights, expand our consciousness, and draw closer to the divine. In this way, the valley becomes a sacred space where seekers of spiritual wisdom learn to navigate the uncharted territories of the soul and find deeper meaning and purpose in their quest for enlightenment.

The Valley is a crucible where the spiritual journey reaches its most challenging juncture. It is here that the seekers, symbolized by the birds, are confronted with profound uncertainties and perplexities, which in turn necessitate a deepening of faith and trust in the journey itself. This enigmatic valley, with its labyrinthine pathways and ever-shifting landscapes, serves as a profound metaphor for the times in life when everything seems unclear and disorienting. It is precisely in such moments that faith and trust are put to the test. The birds, like spiritual seekers, must rely on their inner guidance, the wisdom of their spiritual guide, and their unwavering belief in the transformative power of their journey.

The Valley also challenges the birds to deepen their faith not just in themselves but in the greater cosmic order. It underscores the idea that faith is not a mere adherence to dogma or belief but a living, evolving trust in the unfolding of the spiritual path. When faced with the obscurities of the valley, they must cultivate a faith that transcends immediate understanding, a faith that believes in the ultimate purpose and destination of their journey.

This bewildering terrain compels the birds to rely on their inner compass, their intuition, and their connection with the spiritual guide. It underscores the importance of listening to the still, small voice within and trusting in one's innate wisdom. It is a reminder that even when the external world seems chaotic and uncertain, there is an inner source of guidance that can lead the way.

The presence of the spiritual guide in this metaphorical journey represents the wisdom and guidance that can be found in spiritual teachings, mentors, or the collective wisdom of tradition. The valley encourages the birds to seek solace and direction in the teachings and guidance provided by their spiritual mentor, the Hoopoe, emphasizing the importance of learning from those who have traversed similar paths.

The valley is not a place of despair but an arena for profound transformation. It's a testament to the idea that struggles and moments of confusion are not roadblocks but opportunities for growth. By navigating through the challenges and doubts, the birds are transformed into wiser, more resilient beings, exemplifying the alchemical process of the spiritual journey.

The Valley of Bewilderment, thus, teaches that faith and trust are not passive attributes but dynamic forces that are honed and strengthened through adversity. It symbolizes the transformative power of belief and reliance on inner guidance, urging us to navigate life's uncertainties with courage, conviction, and the unwavering trust that even in the midst of confusion, the path to higher understanding is being illuminated.

Here are some of the key spiritual allegories explained in this valley:

Dissolution of the Ego

The bewilderment encountered by the birds within the Valley serves as a powerful allegory for the disorientation and confusion that often ensue when the ego, with its inherent attachments, rigid expectations, and limited understanding, is confronted by the expansive and profound nature of spiritual truths. This metaphorical valley becomes a crucible wherein the ego's constructs are challenged and eventually dismantled, signifying the imperative to transcend the confines of the ego's comfort zone.

In this narrative, the ego represents the individual's sense of self, replete with its identifications, desires, fears, and prejudices. When these aspects of the self collide with the vast and often incomprehensible dimensions of spiritual truths, bewilderment arises. The ego, conditioned by the familiar and the known, finds itself ill-equipped to grapple with the magnitude of these revelations. The ego clings to attachments and harbors expectations rooted in the material world. It seeks validation and security in the tangible and the measurable. When confronted with spiritual truths that transcend these worldly concerns, the ego struggles to reconcile its attachments and expectations with the greater spiritual reality. This dissonance gives rise to confusion.

The ego operates within the framework of limited human understanding. It relies on rationality and logic, which often fall short when attempting to grasp the transcendent and mystical aspects of spirituality. As the birds navigate the bewildering terrain of the valley, they mirror the individual's journey to transcend their ego's limited understanding and embrace a broader, more intuitive comprehension of spiritual truths.

The Valley of Bewilderment represents the breaking down of the ego's defenses. It serves as a transformative space where the ego's illusions and barriers are dismantled. The bewilderment experienced in the valley compels the birds to confront their own limitations and the inadequacies of their ego-driven perspectives. The valley symbolizes the necessity of moving beyond the ego's comfort zone It is in the disorienting and perplexing moments of the journey that individuals are pushed to relinquish their attachment to the familiar and venture into the unknown. It encourages them to shed the ego's constraints and embrace the broader, more profound dimensions of the spiritual path.

The Valley, in essence, encapsulates the spiritual paradox that genuine growth and enlightenment often require the dissolution of the ego's constructs. It underscores the idea that bewilderment and confusion, rather than being obstacles, are essential stages of the spiritual journey. By confronting and transcending the limitations of the ego, individuals can ultimately attain a deeper, more authentic understanding of spiritual truths and their own inner selves. The valley thus becomes a sacred space where the ego is humbled, allowing the seeker to embrace the boundless expanses of the spiritual realm with greater humility and openness.

Transcending Rational Mind

The distorted paths and reflections within the Valley of Bewilderment serve as a profound metaphorical representation of the inherent limitations of the rational mind when confronted with the mysteries of the divine. In this mystical landscape, the birds' bewildering experiences symbolize the formidable challenge of transcending the confines of the analytical mind to access deeper levels of intuition and spiritual insight.

The valley's distorted paths and reflections vividly illustrate the boundaries of rationality and logical thinking. The rational mind is adept at processing information based on empirical evidence and established patterns. However, when it encounters the profound and ineffable aspects of the divine, it often falls short, leading to confusion and disorientation.

The bewilderment experienced by the birds signifies the pivotal role of confusion in the spiritual journey. It is in these moments of perplexity that the rational mind is challenged and the seeker is encouraged to seek answers beyond the analytical framework. This inner turmoil becomes a catalyst for the expansion of consciousness and the pursuit of deeper spiritual insights.

The birds' journey through the valley represents the arduous task of transcending the analytical mind. To access the profound truths of the divine, individuals must learn to go beyond the linear and compartmentalized thinking of the rational mind. They are urged to explore the realms of intuition, symbolism, and holistic understanding.

The valley invites the birds—and by extension, spiritual seekers—to tap into their deeper intuition. Intuition is often described as a form of inner knowing that transcends intellectual analysis. It serves as a bridge between the finite rational mind and the infinite mysteries of the spiritual world. Embracing intuition allows individuals to navigate the labyrinthine terrain of the valley with greater clarity and purpose.

As the birds grapple with the challenges of the valley, they gradually uncover profound spiritual insights that lie beyond the grasp of the rational mind. These insights are often marked by a sense of interconnectedness, unity, and a direct communion with the divine. They signify the rewards of transcending the analytical limitations and embracing a broader, more holistic perspective.

The Valley of Bewilderment, thus, poignantly illustrates the struggle of the rational mind when confronted with the mysteries of the divine. It emphasizes that confusion and bewilderment are not mere impediments but essential stages in the spiritual journey, propelling individuals to move beyond the analytical mind and access deeper levels of intuition and spiritual insight. Ultimately, this metaphysical landscape becomes a sacred space where seekers learn to harmonize the rational and intuitive faculties, forging a path toward a more profound understanding of the divine and their own spiritual nature.

Faith in the Unseen

The enigmatic terrain of the Valley of Bewilderment presents the birds with a unique challenge that demands they place their trust not only in their external senses but also in their inner guidance and the wisdom imparted by their spiritual guide, the Hoopoe. This allegorical journey underscores the profound importance of having faith in the unseen, the unknown, and the intangible aspects of the spiritual path.

In navigating the bewildering landscapes of the valley, the birds are compelled to rely on their inner guidance, their intuition, and their innate sense of direction. This reliance on inner wisdom is symbolic of the need to trust one's inner compass on the spiritual journey. It highlights the idea that there are dimensions of reality and guidance that cannot be perceived through external senses alone.

The presence of the Hoopoe, their spiritual guide, represents the accumulated wisdom. The birds turn to the Hoopoe for guidance and insight, recognizing that there is value in seeking wisdom beyond their own limited perspective. This signifies the importance of learning from spiritual mentors and tradition in order to gain a deeper understanding of the spiritual journey.

The valley's perplexing nature challenges the birds to have faith in the unseen and the unknown. It pushes them to move beyond the safety of the visible and the tangible and embrace the mysteries that lie beyond. This act of faith signifies the belief that there is a greater spiritual reality that transcends the limitations of the physical world.

The valley's symbolism extends to the idea that true spiritual growth often requires moving beyond external appearances and sensory perceptions. It encourages individuals to see beyond the surface and to recognize that the depths of spirituality are not always apparent to the eye but require a deeper, more profound understanding that comes from within. The allegory ultimately underscores the importance of embracing the intangible aspects of the spiritual journey. It invites individuals to trust in their own inner experiences, revelations, and intuitions as valid and significant components of their path to enlightenment.

The Valley of Bewilderment, hence, becomes a sacred space where the birds learn to place their faith in the unseen, the unknown, and the intangible. It highlights the idea that the spiritual journey is not solely a matter of external exploration but a profound inner quest. Through this allegorical landscape, individuals are reminded that there are dimensions of reality and wisdom that can only be accessed through the trust in their inner guidance and the belief in the spiritual truths that transcend the material world. It is in this act of trust and faith that the true essence of the spiritual journey unfolds, revealing the profound depths of the unseen and the infinite.

Testing the Seeker

The Valley of Bewilderment, within the context of this allegorical journey, takes on a profound significance as it serves as a pivotal test of the birds' dedication, determination, and unwavering commitment to their quest for higher truth and spiritual enlightenment. This mystical valley becomes a symbol not only of the trials and tribulations that seekers invariably encounter on their spiritual path but also of the profound test of their resolve to persevere in the face of bewildering confusion and uncertainty.

The bewilderment and perplexity that envelop the valley test the birds' dedication to their spiritual journey. It is during these moments of confusion that the strength of their commitment is most crucial. The valley, in essence, separates those who are merely curious from those who are truly dedicated to the pursuit of deeper spiritual understanding. The valley symbolizes the challenges and hardships that seekers encounter along their spiritual journey. These trials can take various forms, from doubts and inner conflicts to external obstacles and setbacks. The valley encapsulates the idea that the path to enlightenment is not a smooth and straightforward one but is often marked by moments of confusion and uncertainty.

Navigating the bewildering landscape of the valley requires immense determination and resilience. It is easy to become disheartened or disoriented in the face of confusion, but the birds' ability to press on despite the challenges illustrates their unwavering commitment to their spiritual quest. This resilience is a testament to the transformative power of dedication. The valley also underscores the need for seekers to persevere even when confronted with uncertainty. It teaches that moments of bewilderment are not reasons to abandon the journey but opportunities for growth and deeper understanding. Perseverance in the face of uncertainty is a hallmark of those who are truly committed to their spiritual path.

The valley invites the birds to commit not only to what is known and familiar but also to the vast unknown. It symbolizes the willingness to embrace the mysteries of existence and the divine, even when they seem perplexing and beyond comprehension. This commitment to the unknown is an essential aspect of the spiritual journey. The Valley, therefore stands as a profound metaphor for the tests and challenges that seekers encounter on their quest for spiritual enlightenment. It highlights the importance of dedication, determination, and unwavering commitment to the path, especially when faced with confusion and uncertainty. Ultimately, it is in overcoming these trials that individuals forge a deeper connection with their inner selves and attain the profound insights and wisdom that come with spiritual growth and enlightenment.

Surrender and Letting Go

The bewilderment experienced by the birds as they navigate the perplexing terrain of the Valley imparts a profound lesson in surrender—a lesson that underscores the necessity of relinquishing the need for control, certainty, and immediate understanding on the spiritual journey. This allegorical landscape becomes a poignant reminder that, much like the birds, seekers are called to let go of their attachments to preconceived notions and trust in the unfolding of their spiritual odyssey.

The valley's bewildering nature challenges the birds' sense of control over their environment. Similarly, on the spiritual journey, individuals are often confronted with situations and experiences that are beyond their control. Surrendering the need for control means accepting that there are aspects of life and the spiritual path that cannot be directed or manipulated according to one's desires. The confusion and uncertainty in the valley teach the birds—and by extension, seekers—that the quest for immediate understanding can be counterproductive. The spiritual journey often involves complexities and depths that transcend the limitations of immediate comprehension. Letting go of the need for instant answers allows individuals to embrace the process of exploration and discovery. The valley symbolizes the inherent uncertainty of life and the spiritual path. It reminds us that uncertainty is not to be feared but embraced as an integral part of the journey. By surrendering the need for certainty, individuals can develop greater resilience and adaptability in the face of life's ever-changing circumstances. Just as the birds must navigate the valley without clear direction, seekers are encouraged to release their attachment to preconceived notions and rigid beliefs about the spiritual path. These preconceptions can limit one's capacity for growth and prevent the emergence of new insights and understandings.

Ultimately, the valley calls upon the birds and seekers alike to place their trust in the unfolding of the journey itself. It is a reminder that there is a greater intelligence at work in the universe, guiding and shaping their experiences. Trusting in this process allows individuals to move forward with a sense of faith and openness, even when the path appears uncertain. In essence, the Valley of Bewilderment becomes a sacred space where surrendering the need for control, certainty, and immediate understanding is not a sign of weakness but an act of wisdom and humility. It signifies a shift from a mindset of resistance to one of acceptance, from a focus on destination to an embrace of the journey itself. Through this surrender, seekers can cultivate a deeper sense of inner peace, resilience, and trust in the unfolding mysteries of existence and the divine. It is a profound invitation to let go and allow the journey to lead them to the profound spiritual truths and insights that await.

Transformation through Challenges

The Valley, with its bewildering and enigmatic nature, takes on a pivotal role as a catalyst for the inner transformation of the birds on their spiritual journey. This allegorical landscape becomes a powerful symbol of the challenges and obstacles that seekers encounter, ultimately propelling them out of their comfort zones and into a state of profound inner growth and expansion. The valley symbolizes the challenges and perplexities inherent in the spiritual journey. These challenges are not mere roadblocks but transformative catalysts. In the face of bewilderment and confusion, individuals are compelled to confront their own limitations and preconceptions, pushing them beyond their comfort zones. Just as the birds must navigate the valley's distorted paths and reflections, seekers are called to break free from the status quo. The bewildering landscape disrupts their established patterns of thinking and behaving, challenging them to explore new perspectives and approaches to life and spirituality.

The valley's bewildering nature underscores the necessity of expanding beyond one's limitations. It pushes individuals to transcend the boundaries of their ego, which clings to familiarity and the known. As they grapple with the challenges presented by the valley, they embark on a journey of inner expansion, breaking free from the constraints of their own self-imposed limitations. The valley, thus, becomes a transformative space where seekers undergo profound inner growth. It is in moments of bewilderment and uncertainty that individuals often experience deep shifts in consciousness. They develop greater self-awareness, resilience, and a broader perspective on life's mysteries.

The valley signifies the transition from the comfort of the known to the excitement of discovery. It is a reminder that true growth and expansion occur outside the realm of familiarity. By navigating through the bewildering landscapes, seekers embark on a journey of self-discovery and spiritual awakening. The Valley, therefore, serves as a sacred arena where the birds, and by extension, seekers, are transformed by the very challenges they encounter. It teaches that the spiritual path is not a passive or predictable journey but a dynamic and ever-evolving exploration of the self and the divine. Through the trials and tribulations presented by the valley, individuals are propelled out of their comfort zones, leading to a profound inner metamorphosis that ultimately aligns them more closely with the deeper truths and mysteries of existence. The valley becomes a sacred passage that nurtures and facilitates their growth, ultimately enriching their spiritual journey.

Embracing Paradox

The Valley of Bewilderment, with its perplexing and bewildering nature, brings to the forefront a profound aspect of the spiritual journey —the recognition of paradoxes and the invitation to delve deeper into their inherent mysteries. This allegorical landscape serves as a reminder that seekers often confront concepts and experiences that appear contradictory at first glance, yet reveal profound truths when approached with an open heart and an open mind. The valley's bewildering nature is symbolic of the paradoxes that frequently emerge in the realm of spiritual exploration. These paradoxes can manifest as apparent contradictions, such as the coexistence of light and darkness, doubt and faith, or suffering and enlightenment. They challenge the seeker's conventional understanding and invite them to explore the deeper layers of meaning.

The valley encourages seekers to transcend dualistic thinking—the tendency to see things as either/or, right/wrong, or black/white. Spiritual growth often requires embracing a more holistic perspective that accommodates paradoxes. These paradoxes remind individuals that reality is multifaceted and that deeper truths can be found beyond the limitations of dualistic thinking. Paradoxes are often gateways to the profound mysteries of existence and the divine. The valley beckons seekers to embrace these mysteries rather than attempting to resolve every apparent contradiction. It is an invitation to journey beyond the boundaries of what is known and to explore the boundless realms of the unknown with humility and awe.

Paradoxes can serve as catalysts for a deeper understanding of spiritual truths. When seekers engage with these apparent contradictions with an open heart and mind, they often discover that beneath the surface lies a tapestry of interconnected wisdom. Paradoxes become the stepping stones to profound insights and expanded consciousness.

The valley signifies the integration of opposites—the ability to harmonize seemingly conflicting elements within oneself. This process of integration fosters inner balance and wholeness, allowing seekers to navigate the complexities of life and spirituality with greater ease and grace.

The Valley, in essence, invites seekers to embrace the paradoxes inherent in spiritual exploration as gateways to deeper understanding and insight. It underscores that the spiritual journey is not about erasing contradictions but about finding meaning within them, transcending dualities, and ultimately discovering a more profound and interconnected understanding of reality. By acknowledging and exploring these paradoxes with an open heart and mind, individuals embark on a transformative path that leads to a richer, more authentic experience of spirituality and a deeper connection with the mysteries of existence and the divine.

Navigating the Unknown

The twisted paths and perplexing reflections found within the Valley of Bewilderment serve as a powerful metaphor for the unpredictable and uncharted terrain that often characterizes the spiritual path. This allegorical representation of the journey emphasizes the importance of cultivating courage and resilience as seekers navigate through the unknown, even in the face of uncertainty and confusion.

Just as the valley's twisted paths and reflections defy predictability, the spiritual path is often marked by unpredictability and ambiguity. Spiritual exploration frequently takes individuals into uncharted territories of the self and the divine, where conventional rules and expectations no longer apply. The valley becomes a symbol of the need to navigate the unknown with courage. It encourages seekers to step beyond the comfort of the familiar and embrace the mystery that lies ahead. It reminds them that spiritual growth often occurs when they are willing to venture into unexplored realms of consciousness and understanding. The bewilderment experienced within the valley tests the birds' resilience. Similarly, the spiritual journey often challenges individuals to remain steadfast in their pursuit of higher truths, even when faced with uncertainty and doubt. Resilience becomes a valuable trait, enabling them to persevere through the moments of confusion and perplexity.

The allegory of the valley encourages seekers to approach the spiritual path as an adventure. It reminds them that adventures are not always predictable or straightforward but are filled with surprises and unexpected twists. Embracing this sense of adventure can infuse the journey with a sense of excitement and wonder. The valley symbolizes the idea that growth and transformation often arise from confronting challenges. Just as the birds must navigate through the bewildering terrain to continue their quest, seekers must engage with the challenges presented by the spiritual journey to evolve and expand their consciousness.

The Valley of Bewilderment, thus, serves as a profound reminder that the spiritual path is not a well-trodden road but a meandering and unpredictable journey. It encourages seekers to approach this journey with courage and resilience, recognizing that the twists and turns, as well as moments of bewilderment, are essential elements of the process. By navigating the unknown with an open heart and a fearless spirit, individuals can embark on a transformative adventure that leads them to deeper understanding, inner growth, and a connection with the mysteries of existence and the divine.

Unraveling Illusions

The confusion experienced by the birds as they journey through the Valley of Bewilderment serves as a profound challenge to their perceptions and illusions. This allegorical landscape becomes a powerful symbol, suggesting that the state of bewilderment has the remarkable capacity to unravel the illusions of the material world and, in doing so, open the door to a deeper understanding of the true nature of reality. The valley's bewildering nature disrupts the birds' conventional perceptions of reality. It shakes the foundations of what they have come to understand as "normal" and calls into question the reliability of their sensory experiences. This challenge to perception invites seekers to explore reality beyond the surface and consider that there may be more to existence than meets the eye.

Just as the valley's confusion challenges the birds' illusions, the spiritual journey often requires individuals to confront and unravel the illusions that bind them to the material world. These illusions can include attachments to material possessions, identification with the ego, and a fixation on the external trappings of success. Bewilderment becomes a catalyst for deconstructing these illusions, revealing the transient and ephemeral nature of the material world. The allegory suggests that bewilderment serves as a gateway to a deeper understanding of reality. When individuals are willing to move beyond their illusions and preconceived notions, they open themselves to a more profound exploration of the mysteries of existence. In this state of openness, they may glimpse the interconnectedness of all things, the impermanence of the material world, and the underlying unity that transcends apparent diversity.

Bewilderment can catalyze a profound shift in consciousness. It invites individuals to move from a surface-level understanding of reality to a more profound, spiritual perspective. This shift often involves recognizing the limitations of the ego and the analytical mind and embracing a broader, more intuitive comprehension of existence. The valley, therefore encourages seekers to embrace the unknown. It underscores that the quest for deeper understanding may take individuals into uncharted territory where familiar paradigms no longer apply. This willingness to venture into the unknown is an act of humility and courage, acknowledging that there is much about the nature of reality that remains to be discovered.

The Valley also becomes a sacred space where bewilderment challenges individuals to confront their perceptions and illusions. It encourages seekers to peel back the layers of the material world and delve into the profound mysteries that lie beneath. By unraveling illusions and embracing a more expansive understanding of reality, individuals embark on a transformative journey of self-discovery and spiritual awakening, ultimately leading to a deeper connection with the fundamental truths of existence and the divine.

Unity in Diversity

The disorienting nature of the Valley carries a profound message about the unity of all seekers' experiences, irrespective of their individual paths and backgrounds. In this allegory, the bewildering landscape becomes a powerful symbol, serving as a unifying force that highlights the shared nature of the confusion and challenges encountered on the spiritual journey.

Regardless of one's cultural, religious, or philosophical background, the valley's perplexities remind all seekers that they are bound by a common human experience. The confusion they face is not unique to any specific tradition or belief system; it transcends these boundaries, revealing a fundamental truth about the universality of the spiritual quest.

This allegory beautifully emphasizes that the journey towards truth and enlightenment is a shared endeavor. It underscores that the challenges and bewilderment encountered along the way are part of a collective human experience, uniting seekers from diverse walks of life. In the face of confusion, individuals are encouraged to extend empathy and understanding to fellow travelers, recognizing that they too have wrestled with the same enigmas and uncertainties.

Furthermore, this unity in confusion serves as a source of strength and solidarity among seekers. It fosters a sense of community and shared purpose, reminding individuals that they are not alone on their spiritual journey. Instead, they are part of a larger tapestry of seekers, all navigating the same labyrinthine terrain of the unknown, seeking higher truths and deeper understanding.

The disorienting nature of the Valley of Bewilderment acts as a unifying force, highlighting the shared experiences of all seekers on their spiritual quests. It emphasizes that the confusion and challenges encountered are universal, transcending the boundaries of individual paths and backgrounds. This recognition of unity in bewilderment nurtures a sense of community and mutual support among seekers, reinforcing the idea that the pursuit of truth is a collective and shared endeavor.

In conclusion, the allegories in the Valley of Bewilderment offer a rich tapestry of lessons for those embarking on a spiritual journey. By incorporating these teachings, individuals can transcend the limitations of the ego and rational mind, navigate challenges with faith and resilience, and fully embrace the transformative potential of confusion and uncertainty as they progress towards spiritual realization. It is a journey of profound self-discovery and enlightenment that encourages seekers to continuously evolve and deepen their understanding of the divine and their inner selves.

CHAPTER 16

Valley of Annihilation and Nothingness: Embracing Divine Unity and Practical Wisdom

"The Valley of Annihilation and Nothingness" in Fariduddin Attar's "The Conference of the Birds" is an intense stage of the spiritual journey undertaken by the birds in search of the Simorgh, symbolizing the Divine. This valley represents a crucial turning point where the seekers confront the dissolution of their individual identities and the realization of the ultimate truth.

In this valley, the birds face the annihilating truth of their own nothingness before the Divine presence. It is a stage of profound stripping away – a stripping away of ego, attachment, and all illusions of separateness. The valley is shrouded in the darkness of unknowing, where the mind struggles to comprehend and accept the concept of nothingness. The birds, just like spiritual seekers, are bewildered and disoriented by this stage, for it challenges their entire perception of self.

Here, the birds' understanding of themselves, their desires, and their worldly attachments is shattered. It's a moment of ego death, where they experience the void that remains when all worldly constructs are removed. This nothingness, though initially terrifying, holds the key to the deepest spiritual truths. It's an invitation to surrender to the Divine will and to recognize the unity that exists beyond the limitations of the individual self.

The valley teaches the allegorical lesson that to truly encounter the Divine, one must let go of the ego's grip on identity, to venture beyond the confines of individual existence. It's a paradoxical journey of becoming "nothing" to become one with the Divine "Everything." The lesson is that through annihilation of the self, one finds true existence in unity with the Divine.

The valley of annihilation is a transformative experience that helps the seekers transcend their limited perspectives. Just as a caterpillar must dissolve within the cocoon to emerge as a butterfly, spiritual seekers must dissolve their egos to become one with the Divine. The valley emphasizes the concept of fana, the annihilation of the self in the Divine presence, a concept central to Sufi mysticism.

To embrace the lessons of the valley of annihilation and nothingness, one must cultivate a willingness to let go of ego-driven desires, attachments, and misconceptions of self-importance. It calls for embracing the emptiness within, facing the fears of dissolution, and surrendering to the unknown with trust. This valley reminds seekers that their essence is not bound by individuality but is part of the infinite whole.

Ultimately, embracing the valley of annihilation and nothingness requires a profound shift in perspective. It calls for recognizing that the path to spiritual enlightenment involves relinquishing the ego's need for control and acknowledgment. By embracing this valley, seekers can undergo a transformative rebirth – transcending the ego's limitations and entering a realm of unity and oneness with the Divine, where the illusion of self is replaced with the reality of interconnected existence.

In this Valley, the allegories and metaphors employed serve to convey profound spiritual concepts and experiences that the birds encounter on their journey towards self-realization and divine union. This valley is a pivotal stage that symbolizes the dissolution of the self and the merging of individual consciousness with the ultimate reality.

Candle and Moth Metaphor

The imagery of a moth drawn to a candle flame is used as a metaphor for the seeker's yearning for the Divine. The moth represents the soul, and the flame symbolizes the Divine presence. Just as a moth is irresistibly drawn to the flame and eventually consumed by it, the seeker's ultimate goal is to be consumed by the Divine. This metaphor emphasizes the intense longing and willingness to sacrifice the ego-self in pursuit of union with the Divine.

In many cultures and spiritual traditions, this dance of a moth around a flame captures the essence of deep spiritual yearning. The moth, with its humble and ordinary nature, symbolizes every individual soul on a quest for the Divine, emphasizing that the journey towards enlightenment is accessible to all.

The flame, representing the timeless and radiant Divine force, exists without actively beckoning. Its mere presence is an irresistible allure, much like the Divine presence, which often waits silently to be recognized by those sincerely seeking it.

The moth's erratic flight around the flame mirrors the spiritual journey of a seeker. This dance, filled with moments of closeness, distance, clarity, and confusion, highlights the challenges, doubts, and ecstatic moments encountered on the path towards the Divine. The moth's ultimate surrender to the flame, allowing itself to be consumed, signifies the seeker's readiness to shed ego and limitations, choosing instead to merge with the vastness of the Divine. This act of being consumed symbolizes not a loss but a profound fulfillment.

For those on a spiritual path, the moth and flame metaphor imparts valuable lessons. A genuine yearning is the first step towards the Divine, and the journey, though not linear, is purposeful. Sacrifice, especially that of the ego, is pivotal. The ultimate reward is not material but lies in the unparalleled joy of union with the Divine. The tale of the moth and the flame is a timeless narrative of the soul's pursuit of the Divine and the profound experiences that await those who embark on this journey.

Ocean and Drop Metaphor

Another metaphor used is that of a drop merging into the ocean. This symbolizes the seeker's journey towards unity with the Divine. The drop represents the individual self, and the ocean symbolizes the infinite and all-encompassing Divine reality. The merging of the drop into the ocean signifies the dissolution of the ego-self into the greater whole, where the individual consciousness becomes one with the universal consciousness.

This metaphor of a drop merging into the ocean holds a profound resonance among spiritual seekers, akin to the mesmerizing dance of a moth drawn to the flame. It encapsulates a myriad of profound insights into the human experience and the quest for spiritual understanding.

Consider the individual drop of water, seemingly separate and unique, mirroring the trajectory of an individual soul. In its journey from the skies as raindrops, through winding rivers, and finally into the vast expanse of the ocean, each drop represents the soul's path through life's experiences, challenges, and lessons. This transient existence of the drop, isolated from the larger body of water, serves as a poignant reminder of our ephemeral nature when we perceive ourselves as detached from the Divine source.

Now, shift your gaze to the ocean, with its limitless scope and unfathomable depth. It symbolizes the infinite Divine, a concept that often overwhelms us, reminding us of the majesty and enigma of the Divine. Despite its vastness, the ocean remains constant and undisturbed as innumerable drops merge into its embrace. This reflects the unchanging nature of the Divine, irrespective of the countless souls that find unity with it.

As a drop surrenders its individual identity upon merging with the ocean, it doesn't vanish but, in fact, discovers its true essence. This mirrors the spiritual journey, where union with the Divine doesn't imply obliteration but rather the realization of one's purest essence, transcending individuality. This metaphor imparts invaluable lessons. It underscores the inherent unity of all existence, suggesting that the perceived separation between the individual and the Divine is merely an illusion.

Surrender, much like the drop yielding to the vast ocean, emerges as the path to unity, where letting go of ego and personal desires leads to a profound connection with the Divine. Moreover, while the act of merging can initially appear daunting, much like a drop confronting the boundless ocean, it ultimately offers the revelation that our true essence is far grander than our limited perceptions.

The journey of the drop into the ocean serves as a captivating metaphor for self-discovery and unity, highlighting that in connecting with the Divine, one discovers a deeper connection to the cosmos itself. It encourages us to embrace the unity inherent in all things, transcending our ego-driven sense of self to become one with the vast ocean of existence. Just as the drop becomes part of the ocean, we, too, can merge with the infinite and eternal, finding our truest selves in the process.

Annihilation of the Self

The concept of annihilation, often referred to as "fana" in Sufi terminology, occupies a pivotal and profound place within the mystical realm of this valley. It represents an intense and transformative process that encapsulates the dissolution of the ego-self, severing the shackles of attachments, and transcending the relentless pull of worldly desires. The allegory of annihilation serves as a powerful guide, imparting invaluable wisdom to those on the path of Sufism, revealing the intricate dance between the human soul and the divine.

At its core, annihilation is a spiritual metamorphosis that demands unwavering commitment and dedication from the seeker. It beckons them to embark on a journey within, delving into the depths of their own being, and confronting the formidable stronghold of the ego. This ego, which often masquerades as the guardian of one's individual identity, must be courageously relinquished.

The process of annihilation mirrors the shedding of layers, akin to a snake shedding its old skin to reveal a new, more luminous self. As the ego's grip weakens, the seeker begins to experience a profound shift in perspective. The boundaries that once defined their self are blurred, and the barriers separating them from the divine dissolve. In this sacred transformation, the individual self merges seamlessly into the ultimate reality of the Divine.

This merging, this union, is where the essence of fana finds its culmination. It is a spiritual homecoming, a reuniting of the fragmented soul with its divine source. In this state of annihilation, the seeker becomes one with the universe, their existence intertwined with the cosmic tapestry, and their consciousness harmonizing with the rhythm of creation.

The allegory of annihilation imparts not only a deeper understanding of the self but also a profound sense of liberation. As attachments to the material world wither away, desires lose their grip, and the ego dissipates, the seeker emerges as a vessel ready to be filled with the divine light. The valley becomes a gateway to transcendence, a sacred space where the seeker, having undergone the crucible of fana, stands on the threshold of a profound and enduring connection with the Divine.

The concept of annihilation, or "fana," within Sufi philosophy, is a beacon of spiritual transformation. It guides seekers to relinquish the ego, detach from worldly desires, and merge with the ultimate reality of the Divine. This allegory of annihilation offers a path to profound self-discovery and a transcendent union with the cosmos, inviting all who venture into this mystical valley to embark on a transformative journey towards spiritual enlightenment.

Mirror of Truth

In this mystical valley, the profound wisdom of self-reflection and self-awareness finds expression through the allegorical use of a mirror. This symbolic mirror serves as a potent metaphor that resonates deeply with the seekers, guiding them on a transformative journey of self-discovery and spiritual enlightenment.

Imagine, if you will, standing before a mirror within the vast expanse of this valley. As the seeker gazes into its reflective surface, they are confronted not with a mere physical image but with the depths of their own soul. It is in this contemplative act that the allegory of the mirror comes to life. The mirror, in its pristine clarity, mirrors not the external visage but the internal landscape of the seeker's psyche.

As the seeker delves into this introspective exercise, they are drawn to confront the stark nothingness that arises in the wake of the dissolution of the ego. The mirror reflects not the grandeur of the ego-self but the void that remains once the ego's illusory hold on identity has been shattered. This reflection is a stark reminder of the impermanence of worldly attachments, the transitory nature of desires, and the ephemeral quality of the ego's constructed identity.

The allegory of the mirror serves as an unyielding call for introspection and self-awareness. It compels the seeker to peer beyond the superficial layers of their existence, to acknowledge the inherent limitations of the ego, and to recognize the deeper truth that lies beyond the facade of identity It is in this contemplative act that the seeker begins to unravel the intricate identity of their inner world, seeking to understand the profound interconnectedness of their individual self with the greater cosmos.

In the act of gazing into this allegorical mirror, the seeker embarks on a journey of self-discovery. They come to understand that the dissolution of the ego, while seemingly daunting, is a transformative process that unveils the essence of their true self—the self that transcends the temporal and the material. It is a revelation of the eternal and the spiritual, a revelation of the self's unity with the divine source.

The allegory of the mirror within this mystical valley symbolizes the transformative power of self-reflection and self-awareness. It urges seekers to look beyond the illusions of the ego, to acknowledge the emptiness that follows its dissolution, and to realize the profound truth that lies beneath the surface of identity. Through this allegory, the valley imparts the invaluable lesson that true self-awareness and self-discovery lead to a deeper connection with the spiritual essence of existence, ultimately guiding the seeker toward the path of enlightenment and unity with the divine.

Darkness and Light

Within the mystical confines of this profound valley, a vivid allegory of darkness unfolds, serving as a powerful symbol of the seeker's journey toward enlightenment. This darkness, often described as a place of obscurity and unknowing, represents a pivotal stage in the seeker's spiritual path—a stage where the radiant light of the ego's understanding is deliberately extinguished. In this intriguing allegorical landscape, darkness is not a void to be feared but a necessary crucible in which profound transformation occurs.

Picture the seeker entering this valley, shrouded in the familiar comfort of their ego's understanding, guided by the dim glow of their worldly knowledge. As they venture further into the valley's depths, they find themselves enveloped by an all-encompassing darkness. This darkness is more than just the absence of light; it is the dissolution of their preconceived notions, attachments, and self-imposed limitations. It is a disorientation that challenges the very foundation of their identity.

In this profound obscurity, the seeker experiences a bewildering sense of confusion. The constructs that once defined their self, the attachments that provided a false sense of security, and the desires that fueled their worldly pursuits all crumble into nothingness. The seeker feels adrift, lost in the depths of this darkness, unable to rely on the familiar landmarks of their ego-driven existence.

Yet, it is precisely within this enveloping darkness that the allegory finds its deepest meaning. This darkness is not a state of despair but a sacred passage—an initiation into the unknown, a trial of faith. In the absence of the ego's understanding, the seeker is compelled to relinquish control and surrender to the enigmatic forces at play.

It is in this surrender that the profound transformation takes root. As the seeker lets go of their ego-driven certainties and allows the darkness to permeate their being, they become receptive to the subtle, transcendent light of divine understanding. This light emerges gradually, like the first rays of dawn after a long night, illuminating the seeker's path with profound insights, wisdom, and a deeper connection to the divine.

The allegory of darkness serves as a potent reminder that true enlightenment often emerges from the depths of unknowing and disorientation. It underscores the idea that the ego's understanding, while valuable in its own right, can only take one so far on the spiritual journey. The darkness is a necessary stage, a crucible that purifies the seeker's soul, preparing them to receive the light of ultimate truth.

Within the heart of this mystical valley, the allegory of darkness is a symbol of profound significance. It represents the seeker's disorientation and confusion as the ego's constructs are dismantled, making way for the emergence of divine understanding. The darkness, far from being a void, is a sacred passage where the seeker surrenders to the unknown, ultimately paving the way for the transformative light of truth to shine forth.

Unity of Existence

Deep within the enigmatic confines of this mystical valley, metaphors abound, each one painting a vivid picture of the profound concept of the unity of existence. These metaphors, woven into the fabric of the seeker's journey, serve as windows into the deeper truths of Sufi mysticism. They guide the seeker towards the realization that the boundaries they once perceived – between self and other, individual and universe – are but illusions, ultimately leading to a transformative understanding of the interconnectedness of all existence.

Consider, for a moment, the seeker's path through this valley. As they embark on their quest for spiritual enlightenment, they encounter the concept of annihilation – the dissolution of the individual self, attachments, and desires. This profound process of annihilation is akin to shedding layers of identity, like the layers of an onion, until only the core essence remains. In this process, the seeker becomes aware that the boundaries delineating their self from others were artificial constructs created by the ego. The sense of "I" that once seemed so distinct and separate begins to blur and merge with the greater fabric of existence.

In this allegorical journey, the seeker's realization is akin to the moment a drop of water merges with the boundless ocean. They recognize that the self is not a solitary island but a wave in the vast sea of the cosmos. This insight becomes a profound epiphany, unveiling the interconnectedness of all existence. It is as if the seeker has transcended the limitations of individual identity and stepped into a realm where the distinction between self and other fades away.

The metaphors scattered throughout the valley mirror this essential truth, emphasizing the interconnectedness of all life forms. They are like scattered pieces of a grand puzzle, each offering a unique perspective on the same universal truth. It becomes clear that the seeker's journey is not a solitary one but a shared pilgrimage with all living beings.

This understanding echoes the central tenet of Sufi mysticism, which emphasizes the unity of existence, the belief that everything in the cosmos is interconnected and shares a common essence. The seeker, having undergone the annihilation of the ego-self, becomes a living testament to this truth. They perceive the divine presence in every aspect of creation, recognizing the sacred interconnectedness of all beings.

In essence, the metaphors in this valley serve as signposts on the path to spiritual awakening. They guide the seeker towards the realization that the boundaries separating self from other are illusory constructs, and in this realization, the seeker finds profound liberation. This transformative understanding not only shapes the core of Sufi mysticism but also becomes a guiding light for the seeker's continued spiritual journey, inspiring them to embrace the interconnectedness of all existence with open arms and an open heart. At its heart, this mystical valley beckons the individual towards a transcendent state of unity with the Divine—a state where the boundaries of self and other fade away, and the seeker merges harmoniously with the all-encompassing reality of the Divine.

As the seeker navigates through the valley's teachings, they are reminded of the necessity of embracing the unknown. The allegory of darkness, the mirror of introspection, and the annihilation of the ego all serve as symbolic representations of the seeker's journey into the uncharted territory of their own soul. In this obscurity and disorientation, they are invited to surrender their preconceived notions, relinquish control, and open themselves to the profound mysteries of existence.

Yet, it is precisely within this surrender that the seeker discovers the radiant truth: that the ego's limitations are but transient veils obscuring the eternal reality. The valley's teachings encourage readers to contemplate the nature of self, recognizing that the ego's constructs are merely illusions, and that the boundaries they create are fleeting shadows. What emerges from this transformative journey is a profound understanding of the interconnectedness of all existence—an understanding that lies at the core of Sufi mysticism.

Ultimately, these allegories and metaphors in "The Valley of Annihilation and Nothingness" beckon seekers and readers alike to transcend the confines of individual identity. They invite us to consider the possibility of moving beyond the limitations of the self to experience the boundless unity that exists beyond the ego's grasp. Through this contemplation, the valley offers a path to profound spiritual awakening, where the seeker ultimately merges with the eternal reality of the Divine—a state of blissful unity that transcends the boundaries of time and space, revealing the timeless truth of our interconnected existence.

LESSONS LEARNED FROM THE VALLEY

The lessons learned from the "Valley of Annihilation and Nothingness" in Fariduddin Attar's "The Conference of the Birds" hold valuable insights for integrating spiritual wisdom into our day-to-day lives. Embracing these lessons can lead to profound personal growth and a deeper connection with the Divine.

Letting Go of Ego

"The Valley of Annihilation and Nothingness" imparts a profound and foundational lesson to all who traverse its mystical terrain—a lesson that stands at the very threshold of spiritual awakening. This paramount lesson is the imperative need to let go of the ego, an instruction that echoes through the teachings of Sufi mysticism and has far-reaching implications for one's journey towards self-discovery and divine union.

In the heart of this valley, as the seeker delves into the concept of annihilation, they are confronted with the necessity of relinquishing the ego-self. It is a formidable challenge, akin to shedding a heavy, constrictive cloak that has long veiled the true self. The valley's wisdom emphasizes that the ego, with its incessant demands for validation, control, and superiority, is but a mirage that obscures the path to enlightenment.

In the external world, the ego-driven thoughts and behaviors often manifest in a ceaseless pursuit of recognition and dominance. It seeks validation from others, clinging to the fleeting approval of society. It craves control over circumstances and individuals, attempting to shape reality to its own desires. It strives for superiority, perpetuating a sense of separation and division from others.

However, the valley's teachings urge the seeker to transcend these ego-driven tendencies. It encourages the practitioner to observe those moments when the ego raises its head, to recognize its presence in the mind's inner workings, and to resist its alluring calls. Instead, the valley invites the seeker to cultivate virtues of humility, empathy, and a deep commitment to collective well-being.

Humility becomes the antidote to the ego's relentless quest for self-aggrandizement. It is a quality that allows the seeker to recognize their place within the grand tapestry of existence, acknowledging that their individual self is but a single thread in the fabric of the universe. In this humility, the seeker finds liberation from the ego's constriction and opens themselves to the vastness of divine truth.

Empathy, in turn, bridges the chasm that the ego creates between the self and others. It enables the seeker to step into the shoes of another, to understand their joys, sorrows, and struggles as intimately as their own. Empathy dismantles the barriers of separation and fosters a deep sense of interconnectedness, highlighting the shared human experience that transcends egoic divisions.

The focus on collective well-being is the culmination of this transformative lesson. The valley teaches that as the ego relinquishes its hold, the seeker's perspective expands to encompass not just personal interests but the welfare of all sentient beings. This shift in consciousness reflects the essence of Sufi mysticism—the recognition that the well-being of one is intrinsically linked to the well-being of all.

Ultimately, the first profound lesson gleaned from "The Valley of Annihilation and Nothingness" is a timeless and universal one: the imperative need to let go of the ego. It is a lesson that invites the seeker to transcend the ego's demands for validation, control, and superiority and, instead, to cultivate humility, empathy, and a resolute commitment to the collective welfare. Through this transformative practice, the seeker not only embarks on a journey of self-discovery but also aligns their path with the timeless wisdom of unity, compassion, and interconnectedness—fundamental tenets that illuminate the way toward spiritual enlightenment and divine union.

Self-Reflection

Within the intense teachings of "The Valley of Annihilation and Nothingness," the lesson of self-reflection emerges as a crucial waypoint on the seeker's path toward spiritual enlightenment. This lesson, intricately intertwined with the allegorical use of a mirror, invites the practitioner to embark on a journey of introspection, unveiling the hidden facets of the self and fostering a deep understanding of the inner landscape.

At the heart of this valley lies the allegory of the mirror—a metaphorical tool that serves as a powerful symbol of self-reflection and self-awareness. As the seeker gazes into this symbolic mirror, they are not met with a mere reflection of their physical form, but rather an invitation to delve into the depths of their own consciousness. The mirror beckons the practitioner to set aside moments of quiet contemplation, creating a sacred space for the examination of thoughts, actions, and motivations.

In the process of self-reflection, the seeker is encouraged to be ruthlessly honest with themselves. This honesty is a torch that illuminates the recesses of the mind, revealing attachments, desires, and fears that may have remained hidden in the shadows. It is through this unflinching self-examination that the practitioner begins to understand the barriers and obstacles that hinder their spiritual growth.

Regular self-reflection allows the seeker to identify the ego's persistent attempts to assert itself, to seek validation, and to perpetuate attachments to transient worldly desires. By confronting these egoic tendencies head-on, the seeker gains the insight needed to release their grip on the ego's illusions.

The mirror metaphor emphasizes that self-reflection is not a passive act but an active engagement with one's inner world. It is a process of peeling away layers of self-deception, much like removing layers of dust from a tarnished mirror to reveal its inherent brilliance. As the seeker becomes attuned to the subtleties of their own consciousness, they gradually strip away the veils that obscure their true essence.

Furthermore, self-reflection is a dynamic tool for spiritual growth. It fosters self-awareness, which is the key to unlocking the deeper recesses of the self. The practitioner becomes intimately acquainted with their motivations, aspirations, and the underlying forces that shape their existence. This heightened self-awareness empowers the seeker to make conscious choices, free from the unconscious grip of the ego.

The lesson of self-reflection, encapsulated in the mirror metaphor, is a call to conscious living. It encourages seekers to set aside dedicated time for contemplation, to explore their inner terrain, and to confront the ego's illusions. Through this practice, the seeker gains profound insights into the nature of attachment and desire, ultimately clearing the path for spiritual growth and a deeper connection with the divine.

Self-reflection, thus, stands as a vital component of the seeker's journey. It is an invitation to engage with the mirror of introspection, to delve into the inner recesses of the self, and to foster self-awareness and honesty. By regularly engaging in self-reflection, practitioners illuminate the path to spiritual growth, paving the way for a profound transformation that transcends the limitations of ego and leads to a deeper connection with the divine.

Embrace Darkness and Uncertainty

"The Valley of Annihilation and Nothingness" imparts another profound lesson, one that illuminates the path of the seeker and their journey towards self-realization—the lesson of embracing darkness and uncertainty. In this mystical valley, the recognition of the natural ebb and flow of darkness in life is transformed into a source of wisdom, providing guidance on how to navigate through challenging periods and emerge with newfound self-awareness and growth.

As the seeker traverses this allegorical terrain, they encounter moments of darkness and confusion, mirroring the vicissitudes of human existence. These periods of darkness represent the times when life's challenges and uncertainties cast shadows over the path, obscuring the way forward. It is during these moments that the valley's teachings come to the forefront, reminding the seeker that such experiences are not to be feared or resisted but embraced as opportunities for profound transformation.

The lesson encourages the practitioner to accept the inevitability of darkness in life. Just as night follows day and winter follows summer, moments of obscurity and uncertainty are intrinsic to the human experience. It is within the cocoon of darkness that the seeds of self-awareness and growth can be sown. Much like a seed buried in the earth, it is in these challenging times that the potential for profound inner change lies dormant, waiting to be nurtured and awakened.

Rather than succumbing to fear or despair when faced with adversity or the unknown, the valley's wisdom beckons the seeker to use these moments as fertile ground for deeper self-awareness. In the midst of darkness, when the ego's certainties crumble and the familiar landmarks of life fade into obscurity, the seeker gains a unique vantage point—an opportunity to examine their thoughts, emotions, and reactions in a raw and unfiltered manner.

The allegory of embracing darkness is not a passive acceptance but an active engagement with life's challenges. It invites the seeker to trust that light emerges from darkness, much like the dawn breaks after a long night. By navigating through the shadows with courage and perseverance, the seeker not only emerges stronger but also gains a profound understanding of their own resilience and inner resources.

Moreover, embracing uncertainty fosters a deep sense of humility. It underscores the realization that the ego's need for control and predictability is illusory. In surrendering to the uncertainty of life, the seeker acknowledges their vulnerability and reliance on forces greater than themselves.

Thus, the lesson of embracing darkness and uncertainty from "The Valley of Annihilation and Nothingness" serves as a guiding light on the seeker's path. It teaches that periods of darkness and confusion are not obstacles to be avoided but opportunities for deeper self-awareness and growth. By accepting the natural ebb and flow of life, by trusting that light emerges from darkness, and by embracing uncertainty with humility, the practitioner not only navigates life's challenges with grace but also uncovers the profound wisdom that lies hidden within the shadows, ultimately forging a deeper connection with the self and the divine.

Practice Surrender

In the spiritual journey through "The Valley of Annihilation and Nothingness," the profound lesson of surrender emerges as a crucial and transformative principle. This lesson goes beyond mere understanding; it encourages the seeker to actively integrate the concept of surrender into their daily life, revolutionizing their perspective and approach to the world.

Surrender, in this context, is not a passive resignation but an active and conscious practice. It entails releasing the relentless need to control every outcome and instead entrusting the unfolding of life to higher, divine forces. It is an act of letting go of the ego's illusion of absolute control and embracing the greater flow of existence.

At the heart of this lesson lies the recognition that the ego's incessant need for control often leads to inner turmoil, anxiety, and a sense of separation from the harmonious rhythms of the universe. The valley's teachings encourage the seeker to relinquish this burden of control, to unclench their fists and open their palms to the world, and to cultivate trust in the wisdom of life's unfolding.

Surrender, as taught by the valley, is not synonymous with inaction. It does not imply passivity or resignation in the face of life's challenges. Instead, it invites the practitioner to align their efforts with a sense of divine purpose. It is an invitation to act with intention, dedication, and devotion, while simultaneously releasing attachment to the outcomes of those actions.

In the practice of surrender, the seeker learns to let go of the ego's need to dictate the course of events. They relinquish the illusion of being the sole architect of their destiny and recognize that they are, in essence, co-creators with the universe. This recognition engenders a profound sense of liberation and inner peace, as the burden of the ego's desires and expectations is lifted.

Surrender also deepens the seeker's connection to the divine. It is an acknowledgment that there is a larger, guiding intelligence at work in the universe, a force that is ultimately benevolent and knows what is best for the individual. By surrendering to this higher wisdom, the seeker attunes themselves to the currents of divine grace, allowing them to navigate life's challenges with equanimity and resilience.

Furthermore, surrender fosters humility. It requires acknowledging one's limitations and embracing vulnerability. It is an admission that the ego's claims of omnipotence are baseless and that there is beauty in embracing the unknown, in recognizing that one is part of a vast and intricate tapestry of existence.

The lesson of surrender from "The Valley of Annihilation and Nothingness" is a profound invitation to release the need for control and embrace the unfolding of life with trust and grace. It is a practice that empowers the seeker to align their efforts with a sense of divine purpose, fostering inner peace, resilience, and a deeper connection to the divine. Through surrender, the seeker discovers that true strength lies in letting go, in recognizing the limitations of the ego, and in surrendering to the majestic symphony of existence that unfolds with divine precision.

Seek Unity and Connection

In the spiritual odyssey through "The Valley of Annihilation and Nothingness," the lesson of seeking unity and connection emerges as a radiant gem in the tapestry of teachings. It beckons the seeker to perceive the profound interconnectedness of all existence and to translate this awareness into compassionate actions that resonate with the very heart of Sufi mysticism.

This lesson springs from the valley's core wisdom that the boundaries separating individuals from one another and from the cosmos are illusory veils. In the journey of self-annihilation and self-reflection, the seeker comes to recognize that the essence of self is intimately woven into the fabric of existence itself. This realization, that all living beings share a common spiritual source, forms the foundation upon which the lesson of seeking unity and connection is built.

To practice seeking unity and connection, one must first cultivate a deep sense of recognition—the recognition that every person, every creature, every element of the natural world, is an essential part of the intricate dance of creation. Each entity possesses its own unique thread in the grand tapestry of existence, contributing to the beauty and diversity of the whole.

With this recognition comes an inherent responsibility. The valley's teachings implore the seeker to treat others with kindness, empathy, and respect. It is a call to transcend the ego's divisive tendencies and embrace a worldview that acknowledges the shared human experience. By extending kindness, empathy, and respect to all, the seeker fosters an environment of harmony and mutual understanding.

This lesson also emphasizes the profound impact of our actions. It highlights that each gesture, each word, each act of kindness or cruelty sends ripples through the interconnected web of existence. The valley's wisdom underscores the importance of choosing actions that resonate with compassion, for in doing so, one contributes to the upliftment of not only their own soul but also the collective consciousness.

Furthermore, to seek unity and connection is to actively engage in acts of service and compassion. It is a call to reach out to those in need, to offer support, and to alleviate suffering wherever it is found. These acts of service are not merely altruistic; they are an embodiment of the recognition of unity—a way of acknowledging that the welfare of one is intrinsically linked to the welfare of all.

In essence, this lesson transforms the seeker into an ambassador of unity and connection. It encourages them to weave threads of compassion, empathy, and respect into the tapestry of their daily lives. By living in accordance with these principles, the practitioner aligns themselves with the profound interconnectedness of all existence and contributes to the harmonious flow of the universe.

The lesson of seeking unity and connection from "The Valley of Annihilation and Nothingness", thus, is a luminous guidepost on the spiritual path. It calls upon the seeker to recognize the inherent interconnectedness of all existence and to translate this awareness into actions of kindness, empathy, and service. Through this practice, the seeker not only deepens their connection with the divine but also becomes an agent of positive change in the world, fostering unity and compassion in the umbrella of existence.

Practice Mindfulness

In "The Valley of Annihilation and Nothingness," the lesson of practicing mindfulness emerges as a radiant jewel, casting its brilliance on the path of spiritual awakening. This profound teaching invites the seeker to immerse themselves fully in the present moment, to cultivate an acute awareness of their thoughts, emotions, and surroundings.

Through the practice of mindfulness, the seeker gains a transformative tool for breaking free from the entanglements of the ego and fostering a deeper connection with the divine essence within.

Mindfulness, as taught in this mystical valley, is a state of heightened consciousness. It is a deliberate and non-judgmental awareness of the present moment—a conscious choice to be fully present in the here and now. This practice requires the seeker to set aside distractions, to quiet the mental chatter of the ego, and to immerse themselves wholeheartedly in the unfolding reality of the present.

One of the primary benefits of mindfulness is its ability to liberate the practitioner from the ego's grip. The ego thrives on dwelling in the past or projecting into the future, constantly ruminating on regrets, anxieties, and desires. Mindfulness interrupts this cycle, anchoring the individual firmly in the present moment. It is as if a spotlight is cast upon the ego's illusions, revealing them for what they are—transient and insubstantial.

Through the practice of mindfulness, the seeker becomes an observer of their own thoughts and emotions. Rather than being carried away by the relentless currents of the mind, they watch these mental formations as they arise and pass away. This witnessing consciousness creates a space between the self and the ego, enabling the practitioner to disidentify from the ego's narratives and gain a deeper understanding of their inner landscape.

Furthermore, mindfulness serves as a gateway to a profound connection with the divine essence within. By grounding themselves in the present moment, the seeker can transcend the limitations of the ego and access the deeper wellspring of their being. It is in this state of heightened awareness that the divine presence becomes palpable, like a radiant light that shines from the core of one's existence.

The practice of mindfulness is not confined to moments of formal meditation; it extends into all aspects of life. It encourages the seeker to infuse everyday activities with mindfulness—to savor each bite of food, to immerse themselves fully in conversations, and to approach tasks with a sense of focused presence. In this way, the mundane becomes sacred, and the seeker continually deepens their connection to the divine within and without.

The lesson of practicing mindfulness from "The Valley of Annihilation and Nothingness", ultimately, is a call to awaken to the present moment. It is an invitation to cultivate a heightened awareness of thoughts, emotions, and surroundings, breaking free from the ego's entanglements, and fostering a deeper connection with the divine essence within. Through the practice of mindfulness, the seeker not only gains liberation from the ego's illusions but also embarks on a transformative journey towards the realization of their true self and a profound communion with the divine.

Cultivate Gratitude

In the spiritual journey through "The Valley of Annihilation and Nothingness," the lesson of cultivating gratitude emerges as a radiant virtue that shines light on the path of inner transformation. This teaching invites the seeker to counteract the ego's insatiable appetite for focusing on what is lacking by regularly expressing gratitude for the blessings in their life. Through the practice of gratitude, the seeker not only fosters a sense of contentment but also deepens their recognition of the divine abundance that surrounds them.

Gratitude, in essence, is the art of acknowledging and appreciating the countless gifts that life bestows upon us. It is a conscious choice to shift one's focus from the ego's ceaseless desires and cravings to the present moment, where the richness of existence can be fully savored. This practice requires the seeker to pause and reflect on the many facets of life for which they are thankful.

One of the most profound aspects of gratitude is its ability to counteract the ego's perpetual sense of lack. The ego often fixates on what it does not have, leading to feelings of discontentment, envy, and restlessness. Gratitude, however, redirects the ego's attention to the abundance that already exists. It is as if a veil is lifted, revealing the treasure trove of blessings that may have gone unnoticed in the haze of egoic desires.

Through the practice of gratitude, the seeker cultivates a deep sense of contentment. It is a recognition that, in this very moment, they have enough, they are enough. Gratitude encourages the seeker to embrace the fullness of life as it is, rather than constantly striving for more. It is a conscious choice to savor the present moment, finding joy and fulfillment in the simple yet profound experiences of life.

Moreover, gratitude deepens the seeker's connection to the divine abundance that permeates the universe. It is an acknowledgment that life's blessings are not the result of mere chance but are gifts from a benevolent source—a recognition of the divine grace that flows through every aspect of existence. Through this practice, the seeker aligns their heart with the currents of divine abundance, creating a harmonious resonance with the universal flow.

The practice of gratitude extends beyond mere words of thanks; it manifests in actions and attitudes. It prompts the seeker to express appreciation not only for the tangible blessings but also for the intangible gifts of love, friendship, and spiritual insight. It inspires acts of kindness and generosity, as the seeker recognizes the interconnectedness of all existence and seeks to share their abundance with others.

The lesson of cultivating gratitude from "The Valley of Annihilation and Nothingness" is a transformative practice that enriches the seeker's journey. It counteracts the ego's fixation on lack, fosters contentment, and deepens the recognition of the divine abundance that surrounds us. Through the practice of gratitude, the seeker not only finds fulfillment in the present moment but also aligns themselves with the flow of divine grace, becoming a beacon of light and gratitude in the world.

Practice Detachment

In "The Valley of Annihilation and Nothingness," the lesson of practicing detachment stands as an intense and transformative principle that holds the power to liberate the seeker from the ego's grasp and pave the way for profound spiritual growth. This lesson invites the practitioner to let go of attachments to material possessions, outcomes, and even opinions, creating a space within the heart and mind for a deeper connection with the divine.

Detachment, as taught in this mystical valley, is not a call to renounce the world or become aloof from it. Instead, it is an invitation to balance the world, recognizing that the ego's attachments are the root of suffering and limitation. Detachment means understanding that while one can engage with the world and its offerings, they need not be enslaved by them.

One of the primary aspects of practicing detachment is reducing attachment to material possessions. The ego often seeks security and identity in possessions, believing that the accumulation of wealth and material goods will bring happiness and fulfillment. However, the valley's wisdom teaches that true wealth lies not in the accumulation of objects but in the richness of inner contentment and spiritual connection.

Through detachment from material possessions, the seeker learns to view them as tools rather than sources of identity. Possessions are no longer seen as extensions of the self, but as resources to be used for the benefit of oneself and others. This shift in perspective fosters a sense of freedom, as the seeker is no longer bound by the need to acquire and hoard.

Detachment also extends to outcomes. The ego often fixates on achieving specific results, attaching its sense of self-worth to success and fearful of failure. However, the valley's teachings encourage the seeker to relinquish this attachment to outcomes. Instead, they are invited to focus on the quality of their efforts and intentions, understanding that the true measure of success lies in the alignment with one's spiritual path and inner truth.

In practicing detachment from outcomes, the seeker becomes resilient in the face of life's inevitable ups and downs. They learn to surrender to the divine flow, trusting that whatever transpires is ultimately for their growth and spiritual evolution. This detachment from outcomes allows the practitioner to maintain equanimity and inner peace, even amidst challenging circumstances.

Furthermore, detachment encompasses letting go of rigid opinions and beliefs. The ego often clings to fixed views, creating divisions and conflicts with others who hold different perspectives. The valley's wisdom calls the seeker to release this attachment to opinions, fostering an openness to diverse viewpoints and a deepening of humility and empathy.

Ultimately, the lesson of practicing detachment from "The Valley of Annihilation and Nothingness" is a profound call to freedom and inner expansion. It encourages the seeker to reduce attachment to material possessions, outcomes, and opinions, freeing them from the limitations of the ego and creating space for spiritual growth. Through detachment, the seeker learns to engage with the world with a sense of lightness, allowing them to move through life's challenges and joys with grace and inner peace, ultimately forging a deeper connection with the divine.

Serve Others

In "The Valley of Annihilation and Nothingness," the lesson of service to others emerges as a luminous beacon guiding the seeker on their spiritual journey. This profound teaching encourages the practitioner to engage in selfless acts of service and generosity, transcending the ego's desires and aligning with the interconnectedness of all beings.

Service to others is not a mere moral obligation but a transformative practice that resonates with the core teachings of this mystical valley. It invites the seeker to move beyond self-centered concerns and to extend a helping hand to those in need. In doing so, the practitioner becomes a conduit of compassion, embodying the wisdom that we are all interconnected under the umbrella of existence.

One of the primary benefits of engaging in selfless acts of service is the redirection of attention away from the ego's desires and preoccupations. The ego often fixates on personal gain, success, and gratification. However, when the seeker dedicates themselves to the well-being of others, these egoic concerns naturally recede into the background.

Service to others creates a profound shift in consciousness. It fosters a sense of empathy and compassion as the practitioner actively engages with the joys and struggles of those they serve. This empathetic connection dissolves the ego's illusion of separation, fostering a deep awareness of the interconnectedness of all beings.

Furthermore, selfless service cultivates a sense of humility. It is an acknowledgment that one does not exist in isolation but is part of a vast web of existence. This recognition of interdependence encourages the practitioner to set aside feelings of superiority or self-importance and approach others with a sense of equality and shared humanity.

Engaging in acts of service and generosity also opens the heart. It allows the practitioner to experience the joy that comes from giving without expecting anything in return. This joy is not dependent on external circumstances or the fulfillment of egoic desires; it arises from the act of giving itself, deepening the seeker's connection with the divine essence within.

Moreover, service to others is a tangible expression of the valley's teachings on interconnectedness. It highlights that our actions have a ripple effect, impacting not only those directly served but also the broader human family. By sowing seeds of kindness and compassion, the seeker contributes to the collective upliftment of consciousness and the fostering of a more compassionate and harmonious world.

Thus, the lesson of service to others is a powerful call to transcend the ego's self-centered tendencies and embrace the interconnectedness of all beings. It encourages the seeker to engage in selfless acts of service and generosity, shifting their focus from personal desires to the well-being of others. Through this practice, the practitioner not only deepens their connection with the divine but also becomes a beacon of love and compassion in the world, exemplifying the transformative power of service on the spiritual path.

Embrace Silence

In "The Valley of Annihilation and Nothingness," the lesson of embracing silence stands as a significant and contemplative practice, inviting the seeker to weave moments of stillness and quietude into the fabric of their daily life. This lesson holds the transformative power to facilitate a deeper connection with one's inner essence while transcending the relentless noise of the ego, ultimately fostering communion with the divine presence within.

Silence, as taught in this mystical valley, is not merely the absence of external noise but a sacred space for inner reflection and communion. It is a conscious choice to disengage from the constant chatter of the mind, to quiet the ego's incessant commentary, and to turn inward to the vast, uncharted territory of the soul. Incorporating moments of silence and stillness into one's routine creates a sanctuary for self-discovery and inner exploration. These moments serve as a respite from the external world, a space where the seeker can listen to the whispers of their own heart and the profound wisdom of their inner self.

One of the primary benefits of embracing silence is its ability to transcend the noise of the ego. The ego thrives in the cacophony of constant mental activity, perpetuating desires, fears, and judgments. Silence, however, acts as a gentle but firm hand that quiets this inner turbulence, revealing the spaciousness of inner peace.

Through the practice of silence, the seeker becomes an observer of the mind's fluctuations. They witness thoughts arise and dissolve like passing clouds, recognizing that they are not their thoughts but the consciousness that observes them. This shift in perspective liberates the practitioner from the grip of the ego's narratives and invites them to dwell in the present moment.

Moreover, embracing silence fosters a deeper connection with the divine presence within. It is in moments of stillness that the seeker can attune themselves to the subtle currents of divine grace. This connection is not bound by religious or dogmatic constructs; it is a direct communion with the timeless, formless essence that lies at the core of one's being.

Silence also carries the potential for self-revelation. In the absence of external distractions and egoic noise, the seeker may encounter profound insights, intuitions, and revelations that illuminate the path of self-discovery. It is as if the layers of the self are gradually peeled away, revealing the radiant light of the true self.

Incorporating silence into one's routine need not be confined to formal meditation but can be woven into the tapestry of daily life. It encourages the practitioner to pause and breathe, to savor the present moment, and to cultivate mindfulness. These moments of stillness are like a deep well from which the seeker draws sustenance for their journey.

The lesson of embracing silence is an invitation to turn inward and connect with the inner essence. It transcends the noise of the ego, fostering a deeper connection with the divine presence within. Through the practice of silence, the seeker not only finds inner peace and self-discovery but also communes with the timeless and formless source of all existence, ultimately realizing the divine essence that resides at the core of their being.

Practice Compassion

In "The Valley of Annihilation and Nothingness," the lesson of practicing compassion shines as a radiant beacon guiding the seeker on their spiritual journey. This profound teaching invites the practitioner to extend compassion not only to others but also to themselves, fostering a deep transformation that dissolves the ego's tendencies toward self-criticism and judgment while nurturing personal and spiritual growth.

Compassion, as taught in this mystical valley, is a profound recognition of the shared human experience. It is the ability to empathize with the suffering and challenges of others and to respond with kindness and care. But the valley's wisdom extends this compassion beyond external encounters; it calls the seeker to turn this gentle, healing gaze inward, towards themselves.

One of the primary aspects of practicing compassion is the acknowledgment of one's own imperfections and struggles without judgment. The ego often engages in self-criticism, creating a cycle of suffering and self-doubt. However, the valley's teachings encourage the seeker to dissolve this pattern through self-compassion. It is as if the seeker becomes their own best friend, offering understanding and support in times of difficulty.

By embracing self-compassion, the practitioner begins to recognize that suffering is an integral part of the human experience. They understand that they are not alone in their struggles and that imperfections are not something to be eradicated but embraced as part of the tapestry of life. This recognition leads to a sense of inner peace and acceptance.

Moreover, self-compassion serves as a catalyst for personal and spiritual growth. When the ego's harsh judgments are replaced with self-kindness, the seeker is more inclined to engage in introspection and self-improvement without fear of failure. Compassion becomes the fertile soil in which the seeds of self-growth are sown, nurturing the seeker's journey toward self-realization.

The practice of compassion extends beyond the self to encompass all living beings. It is a call to recognize the interconnectedness of all existence and to treat others with kindness, empathy, and respect. The valley's teachings remind the seeker that every individual, regardless of their background or circumstances, is deserving of compassion.

Compassion is an active force that transforms relationships and fosters harmony. It encourages the seeker to listen deeply, to be present for others, and to offer a helping hand when needed. It is a reminder that we are all fellow travelers on the journey of life, each with our own unique challenges and joys.

Furthermore, practicing compassion is a means of dissolving the ego's divisive tendencies. The ego often creates divisions based on superficial differences, leading to conflict and separation. Compassion, however, transcends these divisions, recognizing the essential humanity in all beings and fostering unity.

Thus, the lesson of practicing compassion is essential to extend kindness and care, both to others and to oneself. It dissolves the ego's tendencies toward self-criticism and judgment, encouraging personal and spiritual growth. Through the practice of compassion, the seeker not only deepens their connection with the divine but also becomes a source of healing and harmony in the world, embodying the transformative power of love and compassion on the spiritual path.

Meditation and Contemplation

In "The Valley of Annihilation and Nothingness," the empowering lesson of engaging in meditation or contemplative practices represents the pinnacle of the seeker's journey. This profound teaching invites the practitioner to delve into the depths of their consciousness, offering a direct and transformative experience of the oneness and unity that the valley symbolizes.

Meditation and contemplative practices, as advocated by the valley's teachings, serve as the bridge between the seeker's inner world and the boundless expanse of the divine. These practices are not mere techniques but profound tools for transcending the limitations of the ego and realizing the timeless truth of unity.

One of the primary benefits of meditation and contemplation is their ability to still the restless fluctuations of the mind. The ego often perpetuates a ceaseless stream of thoughts, desires, and fears, obscuring the underlying reality of existence. Meditation, however, acts as a tranquil pond that reflects the clear sky of consciousness. It invites the practitioner to observe their thoughts without attachment or judgment, creating a space for the emergence of stillness and clarity.

Through these practices, the seeker gains access to deeper layers of consciousness, beyond the ego's domain. It is as if they descend into the innermost chamber of their being, where the spark of divine presence resides. Here, the boundaries that separate the individual self from the ultimate reality of the Divine begin to dissolve.

Moreover, meditation and contemplation facilitate a direct experience of unity and oneness. As the ego's grip loosens, the seeker may experience moments of profound interconnectedness with all of existence. It is as if the veils that separate the self from the world are momentarily lifted, revealing the underlying unity that the valley symbolizes.

These practices also nurture a sense of inner peace and tranquility. The seeker may encounter moments of profound stillness, where the ceaseless activity of the ego subsides, and a deep serenity emerges. This inner peace is not dependent on external circumstances but arises from the recognition of the timeless and formless essence within.

Furthermore, meditation and contemplation serve as a direct pathway to communion with the divine presence. They offer moments of transcendence, where the seeker can experience the profound unity that lies at the heart of all existence. This communion is not bound by religious or cultural constructs but is a direct and intimate connection with the ineffable source of life.

Incorporating these practices into one's daily life extends their transformative power beyond the meditation cushion or quiet retreat. It encourages the seeker to infuse every aspect of their existence with mindfulness and presence. In doing so, the seeker continually deepens their connection with the divine and embodies the wisdom of unity and oneness in their interactions with the world.

The lesson of engaging in meditation or contemplative practices, thus, represents the culmination of the seeker's journey. These practices serve as a direct pathway to the realization of oneness and unity, transcending the ego's limitations and facilitating communion with the divine presence. Through meditation and contemplation, the practitioner not only gains inner peace and clarity but also becomes a living embodiment of the profound teachings of the valley, radiating the transformative power of unity and oneness in the world.

CONCLUSION

Consciously integrating the teachings of the "Valley of Annihilation and Nothingness" into one's daily life is akin to nurturing a sacred garden within the heart. By diligently tending to the seeds of wisdom sown by the valley's teachings, the seeker cultivates a harmonious alignment with these profound principles. Over time, the practices outlined in the valley's wisdom become a wellspring of spiritual growth, a source of deepening connection with the Divine, and a means to experience the unity and interconnectedness that transcend the ego's limitations.

This conscious integration begins with the practice of letting go of ego, the valley's foundational lesson. By observing the ego's tendencies for validation, control, and superiority, the seeker progressively loosens its grip on their identity. As humility, empathy, and a focus on collective well-being become second nature, the ego's dominion wanes, allowing the seeker to embrace the unknown and surrender to the all-encompassing reality of the Divine.

The practice of self-reflection, symbolized by the valley's mirror allegory, is an ongoing journey. By setting aside regular time for introspection, the seeker delves deeper into their thoughts, actions, and motivations. This honest self-appraisal reveals attachments, desires, and fears that may hinder spiritual growth. With each reflection, the seeker polishes the mirror of self-awareness, refining their understanding of identity and truth.

Embracing darkness and uncertainty, as advocated by the valley's allegory of darkness, becomes a way of navigating life's challenges. Rather than resisting disorientation and confusion, the seeker transforms these moments into opportunities for deeper self-awareness and growth. Trusting that light emerges from darkness, they embrace the transformative power of uncertainty, allowing the light of divine understanding to shine.

The lesson of unity of existence, symbolized by the valley's metaphors, continually unfolds as the seeker experiences the annihilation of the individual self. Over time, they realize that the boundaries separating self from other, individual from universe, are illusory. This profound realization deepens their understanding of the interconnectedness of all existence, mirroring the central tenet of Sufi mysticism.

The seeker's conscious integration of these practices culminates in a harmonious and transformative alignment with the teachings of the "Valley of Annihilation and Nothingness." Through the regular cultivation of humility, empathy, and surrender, they become adept at navigating life's uncertainties and discovering the unity that underlies all existence. This alignment, in turn, fosters spiritual growth as they deepen their connection with the Divine.

The valley's wisdom becomes a guiding light, illuminating the path towards greater self-awareness and inner peace. The seeker learns to embrace gratitude for life's blessings, transcending the ego's fixation on lack. They practice detachment from material possessions, outcomes, and opinions, experiencing the freedom that accompanies these releases. Engaging in selfless acts of service and compassion, they become instruments of unity and connection in the world.

The incorporation of silence into their routine allows the seeker to deepen their connection with the divine presence within. Through moments of stillness, they dissolve the ego's noise, accessing the profound wisdom that transcends words. Finally, meditation and contemplative practices become portals to direct communion with the Divine, offering glimpses of the oneness and unity that the valley symbolizes.

In this way, the seeker consciously integrates the teachings of the "Valley of Annihilation and Nothingness" into the tapestry of their daily life. Over time, these practices become an inseparable part of their being, nurturing spiritual growth, deepening their connection with the Divine, and allowing them to experience the unity and interconnectedness that transcend the ego's limitations.

Meeting the Simorgh

CHAPTER 17

Celestial Encounter: The Birds' Meeting with the Simorgh

The culmination of the birds' epic journey brings them face to face with the elusive Simorgh, the ultimate goal of their quest. However, before they can enter the presence of the Simorgh, they must first encounter the Door Keeper, who guards the threshold to the divine realm. This encounter is a crucial part of the birds' spiritual journey, as it represents the final test of their readiness and worthiness.

As the birds approach the threshold, they are filled with awe and trepidation. They have traversed the seven valleys, faced numerous trials, and undergone profound transformations to reach this point. Yet, standing before the Door Keeper, they are keenly aware of their limitations and imperfections.

The Door Keeper, a wise and enigmatic figure, greets the birds with a serene demeanor. His eyes seem to hold the wisdom of ages, and his presence exudes an aura of profound spirituality. The birds, humbled and reverent, bow before him and express their desire to meet the Simorgh.

The Door Keeper, in response, begins to question each bird individually. He asks them about their journey, their motivations, and what they have learned along the way. Each bird, in turn, recounts their experiences, sharing the lessons they have gained from traversing the seven valleys of Quest, Love, Understanding, Independence and Detachment, Unity, Bewilderment, and Annihilation and Nothingness.

The Door Keeper listens intently, his gaze penetrating to the depths of their souls. He acknowledges their efforts and sacrifices, praising their courage and determination. However, he also challenges them, asking whether they are truly prepared to meet the Simorgh and to face the ultimate truth of existence.

One by one, the birds respond with humility and sincerity. They admit their imperfections and limitations but affirm their unwavering commitment to the quest for spiritual realization. They acknowledge that the journey has been one of self-discovery and transformation, and they express their readiness to confront whatever lies beyond the threshold.

The Door Keeper, satisfied with their responses, nods approvingly. He then utters profound words of wisdom, revealing a timeless truth to the birds. He explains that the Simorgh they seek is not a separate entity but a reflection of their own true selves. To their amazement, the Birds discover that the Simorgh is not a separate entity from themselves but a reflection of their own true nature. The Simorgh is a mirror, and when the birds look into it, they see their own faces. In this moment, they realize that they themselves are the Simorgh they have been seeking all along. The name "Simorgh" means "thirty birds," and the realization dawns on them that the thirty birds, who, in the end complete this journey are, in fact, one and the same as the Simorgh. The Simorgh is a symbol of the divine essence that resides within each of them. To meet the Simorgh is to meet the deepest, most authentic part of themselves.

The encounter with the Door Keeper represents the final test of the birds' spiritual journey, a test of their sincerity, humility, and readiness to embrace the profound truth of unity with the Divine. It underscores the idea that the ultimate spiritual realization is not external but internal, a recognition of the divine essence that resides within every soul.

With this realization, the birds are filled with a sense of profound unity and enlightenment. They understand that the external quest was a metaphor for the inner journey of self-discovery and spiritual awakening. The Door Keeper's wisdom has unveiled the ultimate truth – that the Divine is not distant but an intrinsic part of their being.

This profound realization represents the concept of divine unity in Sufism, where the seeker realizes their oneness with the divine and the ultimate truth of existence. The birds come to understand that the journey they undertook was a symbolic one, a journey of self-discovery and spiritual transformation. They had to go through trials and tribulations to shed their ego and attachments, and in doing so, they found their true selves.

The poem concludes with the birds embracing this realization and understanding that they are complete, whole, and united with the divine. They return to their homes, transformed by their journey, and filled with the knowledge that they carry the Simorgh within themselves.

Fariduddin Attar's "The Conference of the Birds" is a beautiful allegorical work that conveys profound Sufi teachings about the path to self-realization and union with the divine. It is a timeless masterpiece that continues to inspire readers with its spiritual wisdom.

BIBILIOGRAPHY

Arberry, A.J. "Mystical poems of Rumi." University of Chicago Press (1968)

Attar, Fariduddin "The Conference of the Birds." Translated by Sholeh Wolpé, W. W. Norton & Company (2017)

Attar Fariduddin, Adamson Kate, "The Conference of the Birds: A Philosophical Religious Poem in Prose" Shambhala, (1993)

Attar, Farid al-Din. "The Conference of the Birds." Translation and commentary by Peter Avery and John Heath-Stubbs. (1979)

Attar, Farid al-Din. "The Conference of the Birds: The Selected Sufi Poetry of Farid ud-Din Attar." Translation by Afkham Darbandi and Dick Davis. (1984)

Attar, Farid al-Din. "The Book of the Sufi's." Translation and commentary by R. A. Nicholson. (1905)

Attar, Farid al-Din. "Bird Parliament." Translation by C. S. Nott. (1928)

Behl, Aditya. "Love's Subtle Magic: An Indian Islamic Literary Tradition, 1379–1545." (2013)

Burckhardt, Titus. "Introduction to Sufi Doctrine." (1976)

Chittick, William C. "The Sufi Path of Love: The Spiritual Teachings of Rumi." State University of New York Press, (1983)

Corbin, Henry. "The Man of Light in Iranian Sufism." Omega Publications, (1994)

Elwell-Sutton, L.P. "Bird Parliament and Other Poems." (1970)

Ernst, Carl W. "Ruzbihan Baqli: Mysticism and the Rhetoric of Sainthood in Persian Sufism." Routledge, (1996)

Helminski, Kabir. "Living Presence: A Sufi Way to Mindfulness & the Essential Self." TarcherPerigee, (1992)

Helminski, Kabir. "The Knowing Heart: A Sufi Path of Transformation." Shambhala Publications, (2000)

Heilpern, John. "The Conference of the Birds: The Story of Peter Brook in Africa." (1977)

Howell et all. "Sufism and the Modern in Islam." I.B. Tauris, (2013)

Lewis, Franklin. "Rumi - Past and Present, East and West.' Oneworld Publications, (2008)

Lewisohn, Leonard. "Farid al-Din Attar's Conference of the Birds: An Inquiry into Its Art and Meaning." (1999)

Lewisohn, Leonard. "Rumi: Past and Present, East and West." (2000)

Lings, Martin. "What is Sufism?" (1975)

Nasr, Seyyed Hossein. "Knowledge and the Sacred: Revisioning Academic Accountability." State University of New York Press, (1999)

Nasr, Seyyed Hossein. "The Garden of Truth: The Vision and Promise of Sufism, Islam's Mystical Tradition." HarperOne, (2008)

Nasr, Seyyed Hossein. "Sufi Essays." George Allen & Unwin Ltd, (1972)

Pourjavady, Reza. "The Foundation of the Community of the Birds." (2006)

Rustom, Mohammed. "In the Valley of Quest: Reframing the Sufi Spiritual Journey in Farid al-Din Attar's 'Conference of the Birds'." Journal of Islamic Literature, (2014)

Sarkarati, Fariborz. "The Concept of Self in Rumi and Attar: The Role of Spiritual Orientation." (1993)

Schimmel, Annemarie. "Mystical Dimensions of Islam." The University of North Carolina Press, (1975)

Schimmel, Annemarie. "The Triumphal Sun: A Study of the Works of Jalaloddin Rumi." (1978)

Smith, Margaret. "Rabi'a The Mystic and Her Fellow-Saints in Islam." Cambridge University Press, (1928)

Wolfe, Michael. "Conference of the Birds: A Seeker's Journey to God." (2010)

Zarrabi-Zadeh, Saeed. "The Conference of the Birds: A Philosophical Interpretation." (2008)

www.ingramcontent.com/pod-product-compliance
Lightning Source LLC
Chambersburg PA
CBHW042115100526
44587CB00025B/4056